THE POCKET BOOK OF
SUCCESS

First published in Great Britain by
New Power Books
2009

www.newpowerbooks.co.uk

A catalogue record for this book is available
from the British Library

ISBN 978-0-9544287-0-9

Printed and bound in Great Britain by
Martins the Printers Ltd,
Spittal, Berwick-upon-Tweed TD15 1RS

Typeset by Solo Typesetting,
Fetcham, Leatherhead, Surrey KT22 9PW

All contents of this book were deemed accurate at the time
of going to press.

For my mother, Anne
Our world is an incomplete one without you

CONTENTS

Introduction

We all measure success in different ways. To me, success is simply achieving my goals and ambitions, and where relevant, reaping the financial rewards that go with them.

I suspect that you, like myself, have read numerous motivational and success publications. I will continue to read them and I hope you will too, because it is such books that inspire me to do the things I do, take the risks I take and to strive on in the face of total adversity. There are few feelings greater than those gleaned from achieving success in your particular project or goal. And let me add this: that high is supercharged with intensity if your project or goal was slammed down and dismissed by others as nothing more than an unattainable dream. Those disheartening and negatively charged words may well echo through your mind, but when success comes, you will have the last laugh.

In my book, you will find no false promises of untold millions, and no so called step by step guidelines to getting rich quickly. Any book promising that is best left on the shelf. 'The Pocket Book of Success' will, however, allow you to tap directly into the thinking of the many great people whose names grace the following pages. I believe this thinking to be right thinking, and therefore the reader could do much worse than to take it on board and try to 're-programme' his or her mind with it.

The truth is, there is no single 'success secret'. There are however numerous attitudes, philosophies and truths which successful people have developed to the point that they live their lives by them. So as a whole, the big 'success secret' is to think in these ways. In a nutshell, successful people have developed a particular state of mind. Your primary objective should be to develop that for yourself. Without it, you will not succeed.

There is another state of mind that has been, to all intents and purposes, an essential ingredient for success with many entrepreneurs and that is the word 'fun'. Richard Branson and Donald Trump are two of the majors in that world. It would appear that for them, if it isn't fun, there is no point. I cannot endorse that view enough. I simply don't do it in the first place if I can't see the fun element. Fun and passion gives you unimaginable energy and drive. When it comes to selling, anyone can sell to a certain extent, but if they really enjoy the job and have total belief in the product or service – and there is a market for it – the sales will rocket.

I have tried to quote mostly from people who are self made. With few exceptions, I have excluded those people who come from privileged backgrounds and those whose wealth is inherited. I am not saying there is a problem with such money, but of course the real value of inheritance is in what you do with it.

With this book you should be able to open at almost any page and find instant inspiration. No matter what situation you are in, be it a meeting you are about to enter, a client you are about to visit, an interview for a new job which you are about to attend, or any other given situation you find yourself in, you should be able to apply or adapt at least one part of nearly any page to your situation in some way. I'll give you an example. Some years ago I was being interviewed by the sales director for a negotiator's position in an estate agency. I had no previous experience in that field and this was pointed out to me by the interviewer. Obviously I didn't have the benefit of a book like this so I simply said, *"Well, I believe that the principles of sales and negotiation are universal and transcend all business, the only real variable is the product or service."* I went on to cheekily suggest that the company also believed it, otherwise I would not have even been granted an interview. The interviewer wrote that down and his next question was, *"When can you start?"*

Motivational publications play a valuable role in creating positive energy and thinking in everyone who reads them. However, I have always felt that too many of the available titles contain too much in the way of 'filler material' which the reader has to sift through in order to get to the hard facts, the tips, the pointers and the quotes, which more often than not are too few in number. It was a need to draw them out and introduce the inspirational philosophies of some of the world's most successful entrepreneurs and prominent people, both past and present, that were some of the reasons behind writing 'The Pocket Book of Success'.

I have met so many talented people who have great ideas and beautiful dreams that turn into catastrophic failures, even horrible nightmares for many reasons. Perhaps they couldn't convince others to help them or they lacked confidence and were too afraid of failure to take a little leap of self faith now and then. Maybe it was because they didn't think things through or established whether or not there really was a market for their product or service. Perhaps they got everything right except costs and pricing. Whatever the reason, I somehow felt an affinity with those people. They needed inspiration and motivation, just as I did, but couldn't find a compact source, an all-in-one handy little guide, to save all that trawling through millions of internet pages and hundreds of books. So this book is for people like them – are you one those people?

Perhaps you haven't even formulated an idea yet but feel a need to improve your life in some way.

Maybe you feel that the route you would like to take is to start a business, or perhaps rise up in the company you work for, and you need that extra boost of motivation and inspiration. It could be that you have in the past been a successful entrepreneur but somehow you have lost focus or direction and the solution may well be to go back to basics to find yourself again. If this sounds like you then '*The Pocket Book of Success*' is for you.

I've included some of my own experiences, modest achievements and some of my failures too. They're not there because I need to prove myself in any way, they're there as examples. But what is important is that if we have to prove anything, it is to ourselves that we need to prove it.

As I came across the various pointers, tips and quotes that I have included in the following pages, I found myself newly inspired. It was like a fresh burst of energy charging me up. I took a journey to places in my own mind that I had never been to before. Want to take a ride?

Chapter 1

In the Beginning,
there was the Idea!

The title of this chapter was an idea I had, just like this book was an idea. The title has, I admit, a biblical undertone, though I'm not particularly religious, but dare I suggest that the bible got it wrong – the opening line of the bible should have been *'In the beginning there was God, and one day God had an idea'*.

Trust me when I tell you that every human manufactured product the world over (and possibly divine creation, if you believe in that sort of thing), all component parts, every service available, every shop and business in every high street, and the high streets themselves, every book, piece of recorded music, every movie ever made, everything human created everywhere, began as a solitary idea. Talk about ideas, talk about big ideas. From them come great creations!

> *Great people talk about ideas.*
> *Average people talk about things.*
> *Little people talk about other people.*
> **Author unknown**

If you're going to dream, dream big!
> **Peter Jones (Dragons' Den)**

Most good ideas sparkle in simplicity. So much so that everyone wonders why no one ever did that before.

Estée Lauder

I dream for a living.

Steven Spielberg

I have found that ideas come to you when you have a great desire to find them. The mind becomes a watchtower from which we look out for any incident that might excite the imagination. Music, a sunset for example, can germinate an idea.

Charlie Chaplin

I don't think you can change the world by attacking it. I think you have to have ideas. Ideas change the world because ideas are subversive.

Vivien Westwood

There's not much difference between a fantasist and a visionary. We all have dreams and without dreams in business I don't believe you can be successful. The trick is to turn those dreams into reality. You have to have passion for that dream. It's got to be something you're going to enjoy, otherwise it's highly unlikely that you will achieve your goal. You must not however, fall into the trap of ignoring the facts and deficiencies in your idea. That's where a lot of people trip up – they lose sight of the bigger picture and ignore the failings of the idea. Making

14

£100m is easy. Making your first £1m is the difficult part. You have got to be passionate about your idea. It is imperative that you have an idea you really believe in, and you also have to be absolutely determined you can make it work. But if you don't attempt to do it, it will never happen. Don't let your idea be the one that got away.

Theo Paphitis (Dragons' Den)

Few people really think and use their imagination more than two or three times a year. I have made an international reputation for myself by thinking two or three times a week.

George Bernard Shaw

I had total faith in the idea of the shop. I knew that the idea of selling skin and hair care products made from natural ingredients was a good one. When enough people tell you what a good idea it is, it helps to build your confidence which is another vital ingredient for success.

Anita Roddick (on The Body Shop)

Ideas, ideas, that's all we need!

Helena Rubenstein

Every person with an idea has at least two or three followers.

Brooks Atkinson

A stand can be made against invasion by an army. No stand can be made against invasion by an idea.

Victor Hugo

One sound idea is all you need to achieve success.

Napoleon Hill

The real problem is not whether machines think, but whether people do.

B F Skinner

Most people would rather die than think. In fact they do so.

Bertrand Russell

More gold has been mined from the thoughts of people than has ever been mined from the earth.

Author unknown

One's mind, stretched to a new idea, never returns to its original dimensions.

Oliver Wendell-Holmes Sr

The best way to have a good idea is to have a lot of ideas.

Irvine Robbins

Observe the masses then do the opposite.

James Caan

There is not enough darkness in the whole world to put out the light of one small candle.

Robert Alden

Wealth is the product of a person's capacity to think.

Ayn Rand

The thoughts that come often unsought, and as it were, drop into the mind, are commonly the most valuable of any that we have.

John Locke

An individual who has a mind and knows it, can always beat ten people who haven't and don't.

George Bernard Shaw

Imagination is more important than knowledge.

Albert Einstein

Whatever the mind can conceive and believe, it can achieve.

Author unknown

I'll let you into a little secret – despite having made a fantastic living from my business ventures, I've never had an original idea in my life. Always remember that because something is innovative or uses leading-edge technology doesn't necessarily mean it's going to make pots of money. Many inventions that were thought to be technologically brilliant and ideas that seemed to have enormous merit never made their inventors a penny piece. Just as the road to hell is paved with good intentions, so the road to bankruptcy is paved with good ideas. There are many good ideas put to us on Dragons' Den that we don't invest in purely because they ain't going to make anyone any money.

Theo Paphitis

There are two ways of making a good living. One is the result of hard work, and the other, the result of imagination, which of course requires work too. It is a fact that labour and thrift produce a competence, but fortune, in the sense of wealth, is the reward of the person who can think of something that hasn't been thought of before. In every industry, in every profession, ideas are what America is looking for. Ideas have made America what she is, and one good idea will make someone what they want to be.

Bruce Lee

Authors note:
Make no mistake – absolutely anyone can create a huge fortune from a single idea with little or no start up money – age, race, background and disabilities have nothing to do with it. Do not listen to anyone who tells you otherwise. The history of the world is overflowing with so called no hope cases going from rags to astounding riches!

Duncan Bannatyne started business at the age of 30 because, as he says, he couldn't get a proper job that would pay and he wanted to get married etc. He worked in a bakery for a while and would go to car auctions to buy and sell for profit. One day he bought an ice cream van. Four years after that he had six of them and a cool turnover of £300,000. Now he's worth £300 million. That first ice cream van cost £450.

John Hargreaves, the son of a Liverpool docker and founder of Matalan Discount Stores, left school at the tender age of 14 and had the idea of selling Marks & Spencer seconds from a stall. A trip to the US brought him the idea of the discount stores after seeing the success of Wal-Mart. His estimated worth is around £2 billion.

But you don't need to start at the age of 14:

Ray Kroc decided to buy a single hamburger stall from the McDonald brothers and turned it into the colossal fortune behind the golden Ms you see all over the world – he was 50 years old when he bought that stall.

Colonel Sanders was past most people's retirement age when he hit on the idea of Kentucky Fried Chicken.

Mark Dixon, the son of an Essex based Ford mechanic, left school at 16 and went backpacking.

He then went through various jobs including nightclub waiting. He started saving, bought a bakery for £10,000 sold it for £800,000 and eventually founded Regus Business Centres, an idea which came to him after a struggle to find an office in Brussels. Regus leases offices on a short term basis through more than 300 centres worldwide and Dixon is worth far in excess of £1 billion.

In 1923 **John Moore** stood outside Liverpool's soccer ground and started selling coupons – and today, we have all heard of Littlewood's Pools, an empire which is worth far in excess of £1 billion.

Graham Wylie came up with the idea of convincing companies to put all their accounts onto computer – Sage, the software firm was born and had you or I had the idea of investing just £100 in shares when Sage went to the stock market in 1989, we would have made well over a million pounds. The company value skyrocketed from £21 million to £10 billion in just 12 years.

YAHOO!!!! is what you would be shouting too if you had Google and Microsoft each trying to throw $40 billion at you to buy your company. Well that's what happened to **Jerry Yang** and **David Filo** who created their search technology for their own personal use. The famous web portal was originally only a side project between the two when they were college students because there was no easy system to find information on their school network – they created a 'crawler' that could find what they needed.

David and Richard Darling, two brothers who began designing games in a garden shed have amassed a personal fortune of over £500 million from their very well known computer games company – Codemasters. It sometimes pays to keep it in the family.

Anne Wood had an idea which she decided to call Ragdoll Productions. In the early days Anne sat in her living room with just two employees. Who would have predicted that a group of performers dressed in bright furry costumes, known affectionately to all as the Teletubbies, would have launched that little home based enterprise into a £150 million empire.

Sir Donald Gosling hit on the idea of charging 6p a day, after the Second World War, to drivers to park on ground where buildings had stood before they were bombed. NCP car parks is a name all drivers know today and though they are not exactly the cheapest parking facilities around, they gave Sir Donald and his partner and NCP co-founder Ronald Hobson, nearly £300 million each when they sold the company.

Alan Michael Sugar (Trading) – became Amstrad amongst other great things. He began by selling car aerials from a van.

And **Bill Gates'** idea may well have been to own the planet – whatever it was, he very nearly does – in recent times his worth has fluctuated between $50 and $100 billion dollars, but who's counting? Perhaps one of the richest men in the world became so from the seed of a solitary idea.

Have you heard of **Tetra Pak** – no? Well that's milk cartons to you and I. Those cartons we all use, resulted in a multi-billion pound fortune for the Rausing family whose Swedish grandfather came up with the idea and founded the company. Today, Dr Hans Rausing's share of the family business, together with other investments, is worth over £6 billion.

Jason Fry worked for a tour operator that went bankrupt. He decided to set up his own business – a travel website called Alpharooms. He worked alone from a box room in Sheffield. He now employs a hundred staff and turns over several million pounds a year whilst processing hundreds of thousands of hotel room bookings annually.

There was a shop fitter called **Anthony Sherlock** who started out as a 'man with a van' business – he now runs Probuild Birmingham with a £5m turnover, 70 staff and he can count major retailers like Sainsbury's and Tesco as his clients.

In 1991 **Brendan Flood** remortgaged his home for

£20,000 and formed Modus Properties. It runs property development schemes nationwide and has clients such as Debenhams and M&S. Profits exceed £7m.

Gerard Abbot Drake and **John O'Leary** remortgaged their homes to start Go Interiors which now has a multi million pound turnover.

Derek Raphael started his metals trading business without any outside money. His company's turnover at last check was well over £300m.

Henry Goldenberg also started with nothing. He founded HQ UK hair and beauty products firm. He says, *"We didn't need to buy stock. From the beginning we fulfilled orders for professional hair products from the shelves of our salon, and business grew from there."*

And last but most certainly not least – **Richard Branson** – no longer a Virgin to business.

Someone once came up with a seemingly obvious idea called the **skateboard.** Many years ago a man used his imagination and came up with an idea that is probably the most famous brand name in history – you may have heard of it, it's a drink called **Coca Cola.** Remember the opening paragraph of this chapter? Read it again!

Bear this in mind: **Understand why you are taking action on an idea!**

Tim Smit the co-founder of the Eden Project says, *"Do something that you feel passionate about because if you feel passionate about it, you'll understand the rhythm of it and you'll know whether it's a good or bad idea. A lot of people come off the rails because they think that something is a good business idea but it doesn't actually motivate them as an idea except for the making of money. I've seen many successes by people passionate about an idea but many more failures by people obsessed with making money."*

Now stop, just for a moment, and look around the room or wherever you are at this time. How many ideas, simple or complex, can you see? There are probably hundreds.

In your hands now you are holding numerous ideas! Many processes, materials and inventions were utilised to create this book and to distribute it – all ideas!

How do you come up with great ideas? No one really knows the answer to that with certainty, and wouldn't it be a great business if you could get paid to teach people how to come up with ideas! Well people get paid to actually come up with ideas all the time, don't they? So, why not? It's most likely that ideas originate in the subconscious mind, which is the all powerful and creative part of our minds. Obviously, as it is a sort of computer, if you fill it with the bad and the negative then that is what it will churn out in return. I will suggest that you come up with ideas all the time. It would be a good idea for you to start by taking stock of your strengths, things that interest you most, things that you have a particular talent for. You don't have to be the best, better than average is ok. Think of ways to improve something you do, or something you use, be it a product or service. What bothers the hell out of you is likely to have the same effect on others – create a solution. Whatever you do, keep it simple and keep it fun. People who don't enjoy what they do rarely become really good at it. Some people find fun in making the deal itself. Some just can't get enough of deal making. If you change your mind-set and start to think like an entrepreneur then I believe ideas will develop in your mind faster and in greater abundance. Everyone has had an experience where they came up with the solution to a problem or they came up with a way of doing something they wanted to do – they came up with an idea. Could that idea be the solution to a problem that many people experience – therein could be the seed of a great business.

There's a great deal of information available about the subconscious mind, its power in the creation of great ideas and the importance of spending time in silence, stillness and solitude, away from the noise of everyday life and work, to allow the conscious mind to become calm so that we can 'hear' what is happening in the subconscious mind. I'll try to condense it into a couple of pages.

Edison said, *"when you become quiet, it just dawns on you."*

I usually come up with my best ideas or solutions to problems when I'm away on holiday. When I go on holiday I leave all thoughts of work and business behind. There is no space for it in *my* 'suitcase' and there should be no space for it in yours either.

If you can get away, even on a cheap break, then do it. If you can, pick somewhere warm, quiet and scenic – preferably abroad (well let's face it, warm weather is going to be a little tricky to find in the UK).

Why? Because at home you are too close, geographically, to your worries and problems, and in my experience there is great psychological advantage to being as far away from those issues as possible. When you are on holiday, sometimes it takes a few days to switch off but you eventually do when you soak up the slower pace of life at your chosen destination. But you absolutely must switch off! That means total 100% cut off. No half measures. No newspapers – you don't need to keep in touch with what's happening in the UK, and it doesn't matter what the latest football score is, so no TV for you. Disassociate yourself with everything that connects you mentally with the home country, especially work, problems and business issues etc.

Don't consciously try to come up with new ideas or solutions to problems. 'Plant the seed' consciously, eg, the need for solutions, ideas or whatever it is, and do this before you leave. Then put it all out of your mind, completely. Forget about it. I promise you if you really switch off, after a few days you will begin to feel totally refreshed, but I'm sure you have already experienced this renewed burst of energy when you have been on holiday. That feeling is exactly what I am talking about. You feel like you can take on the world!

Some people can't get away abroad for whatever reason, and if that's you, then at least get as far as you can from towns and cities and even large numbers of people. There is no tranquillity to feed your peace of mind in those locations. Get away somewhere really quiet with clean air. Go for long cycles or long walks. You must take time out on your own, away from traffic jams, away from screaming kids, dogs barking and mobile phones ringing and away from all negative influences like debt and bills – anything that puts you under pressure and brings you down.

As I understand it, this practice works because by switching off and breaking away, the conscious mind becomes free of the external issues and negative din of life and that stressful rat race that most people struggle to live amongst. This effectively allows the subconscious mind to breath. It allows us to then 'hear' what is happening in our subconscious and as I have said, therein are huge reserves of creative power and therefore, the solutions to just about everything. James Caan of BBC Dragons' Den was recently featured on television taking time out to switch off – okay he is able to do it in a degree of style – on a very nice boat on the French Riviera, but he made it clear that even with his success and financial security he needed to cut himself off from business and recharge his mind from time to time.

So, with your mind refreshed and a great idea bursting out of you, what are you going to do? Allow me to make a suggestion........

Chapter 2

ACTION!
ACTION!
ACTION!

Get into action and do it now! For every idea you have, a thousand other people could have thought of it before you. You must therefore act NOW, and seize the moment. Those who take action win! If only you knew how many great ideas I have had, only to make the shocking discovery months or years later that someone else had the same ideas and took action on them and made a fortune. An early draft of '*The Pocket Book of Success*' sat on a shelf for three years. I had, what I would call, a period of inaction, or to be more precise, a phase of big talk, no action. Then one day I came across the words of **Alfred North Whitebead** who said, *"Ideas won't keep, something has to be done about them"*. The book you now hold is one of the results. Learn from other people's mistakes, learn from my mistakes – I did. Don't waste time. Make every second count! Have you ever been in the situation where you are struggling to get a job? You write dozens, if not hundreds, of letters and send your resume to everyone, but you get don't even get an acknowledgement. If they won't employ you, take action and employ yourself!

Duncan Bannatyne says, *"Abandon the pub. You can't spend your evenings drinking and playing* darts – time is money. You can't buy it so why would you want to waste it?"

And **Deborah Meaden** says, "*The first thing you need to do is create a business plan. There's a big chasm between a bright idea and actually creating a business. The important thing about a business plan is that it's a map for yourself, it's not for anybody else, it is your map that says that's where I'm going to go, this is the map that says how I'm going to get there. So make sure that you're not just doing it for external reasons you're doing it for yourself.*"

Peter Jones on research and feasibility, "*You need to research your idea so that you've covered off not just all the competition in the market but you've checked and double checked whether your idea is likely to work or not. So many people today start up a business because they do it on the back of a whim. They need to research the market, they need to discuss how feasible it is and then ask questions. How am I going to get out of the business? Who am I going to sell it to? Who are my competitors in the market? Who are my suppliers? How much money do I need to start the business? How will I market the company? There's a lot to consider but research and feasibility are fundamentally important when starting a new business.*"

There's something else to add to the comments of the Dragons. Research does not mean asking your best friends or mother and father if they think your product is a good idea. So many people say things like, *"well everyone I've spoken to thinks it's a great product."* Really? How many have they bought or ordered? If you want advice, you need impartial advice. You need to analyse your idea from a cold and critical standpoint. If there are flaws or potential pitfalls in your idea, think about cost effective solutions to those problems because by doing so you will often find that you have discovered a way to improve your business.

I'm going to go off track just for a moment and talk about 'smoking' You'll see the relevance shortly and also how you can adapt and apply this information to other situations.

Many companies allow significant time wastage through smoking. Walk past almost any office block at any time of day and you are likely to find a number of staff standing outside smoking. If a hundred people do that on company time even five times a day for five to ten minutes on each occasion, that's between 40 and 80 hours of company time per week up in smoke. What does an hour cost a large company, or any company for that matter? I would have thought a lot of positive action could be taken in that time.

We all know that tobacco companies are actually selling an addictive drug, and they are doing this legally because governments allow them to. But what is relevant here for our purpose is that they have succeeded in selling to a global market through one of the most powerful methods of advertising known – free advertising. Not so many years ago, it seemed that everyone appearing in a movie smoked, you rarely if ever, saw the brand that they smoked so there was no issue of product placement. What's important here is that the viewing public saw this as fashionable, and emulated it accordingly. In this day and age less people smoke in some countries such as Britain, but people are still influenced by seeing other people smoking and therein the tobacco companies have again obtained advertising for free.

Try to apply and adapt this concept by thinking up ways of getting free advertising and word of mouth marketing. Could you, for example, get into action by offering a service or product to your neighbours, perhaps even offer the product or service at an introductory price? If it is a good product or service that people need or desire, the word will spread, but if it doesn't work the cost of trial on a few will be a lot less than failure on the many.

Just returning to the smoking example for the moment, if you and your partner smoked twenty cigarettes a day each at current prices, that's £3500-£4000 per year!! How many websites selling your great ideas could you set up with that money? I can tell you that you can set up at least eight great websites. In other words your burnt cigarette money could make YOU millions instead of making a tobacco giant richer and giving yet more taxes to the government. In addition to the health benefits, giving up smoking is positive action with other advantages. If you smoke and say you'll give up next month or next year, you are deceiving yourself and denying yourself valuable cash for your business.

If you smoke, GIVE UP NOW! Seriously, what's stopping you? Fear of cravings, or withdrawal symptoms? Let me tell you that those feelings are pathetically insignificant compared to not knowing where your next meal is coming from or when you have to borrow money to feed your children – I know, I've been there and I did smoke cigarettes. I'll tell you something else – not so long ago someone had to borrow money to go to his mother's funeral because he failed to get into **action** against someone who withheld money from him for sales commissions, at a time when he desperately needed it. That, my friend, is a historical fact for the person I speak of is again, me, and I will never forget those events. In respect of what I have learned from these experiences and what action I took as a consequence, it is this: as long as I live I will never allow anyone to walk over me again. More importantly, I learned that **only** by **taking action** would I reach a position where <u>I</u> am in control of my life and not someone else!

Now think about what else you could give up or cut down on that's costing you a lot of money but has no real benefit to you. By cutting it out you could use that money for a greater purpose.

Here's a lateral thought: Cut out an empty room! Do you own a house – can you rent out a room or two? Well lo and behold you just brought in £300 - £500 per month – per room! Is that your mortgage covered, or your bills paid, or simply money to get a business going ???

Are you asking yourself what business should you get into action on? And what action do you need to take to set up a business? Well Deborah Meaden from Dragons' Den talked about a business plan. You have an idea, so some action to be taken is research, feasibility and a business plan. If it all checks out, your next action will simply be to follow your plan. The right answers to the questions about what business to go into could be worth enormous fortunes.

Every business is different. Certainly the basic principles are the same. In a nut shell, you buy in or produce a product at one price (cost) and sell it at a higher price. The difference between cost and 'price sold at' is the margin or gross profit – buy low, sell high! Same principal with a service. There will be costs and there is the profit margin. Obviously there are other factors to take into consideration and there may be a multitude of them involved depending on the complexity of your business structure. It could be argued that the simpler the business the better for you and your clients. Is it easy to set up a business? It can be unbelievably easy to set one up. That will depend on what you are trying to do. In fact I just gave you an idea, renting a room in your house. Now that could become a business – you take action by setting up an agency renting rooms in other people's houses, perhaps starting with rooms in friends' and neighbours' houses? Find out by doing research – put a plan together – act on the plan and suddenly you're in the property rental business!

Once upon a time I wanted to do some photography work. Okay, I had the talent and I had a good camera. I put an ad in the Yellow Pages and the phone began to ring. Obviously that's a condensed version of the story as there were various other elements, but on a basic level that's what happened.

So what motivates you into action? Here's what **Simon Woodroffe** of 'Yo Sushi' and **Dragons' Den** says, "*I never got up at four in the morning because I wanted to be rich. I got up at four in the morning from the fear of being very poor.*"

Peter Jones says, "*So many people talk about doing something or say 'what if'. They don't actually get up and do it.*"

WHO DARES WINS!

Motto of the Special Air Service

Ideas won't keep, something has to be done about them.

Alfred North Whitebead

Above all, try something.

Theodore Roosevelt

When in doubt, jump.

Malcolm Forbes

To be successful you have to be out there, you have to hit the ground running.

Richard Branson

Intellectual property has the shelf life of a banana.

Bill Gates

Deliberation is the work of many. Action, of one alone.

Charles De Gaulle

Entrepreneurs cannot stand still. If they do, the laurels they choose to sit on will attach themselves to their backsides, engulf them and turn them into nothing but inactive vegetation.

Victor Kiam

Action is eloquence.

William Shakespeare

Those that are superior act before speaking and then speak in accordance with their actions.

Confucius

While the worriers are worrying, the planners are planning and the accountants are figuring out why we can't afford it, I'm busy getting started.

Walt Disney

The first one gets the oyster, the second one gets the shell!

Andrew Carnagie

Only do the thing and you will have the power.

Emerson

The secret of getting ahead is getting started. The secret of getting started is breaking your complex overwhelming tasks into small manageable ones, and then starting on the first one.

Mark Twain

The only people who don't make mistakes are those who do nothing, and that is the biggest mistake of all.

Dr William Reilly

Life is too short to be little, so why do so many people sit around waiting for the right time to act.

Benjamin Disraeli

Action makes more fortunes than caution.

Vauvenargues

All glory comes from daring to begin.

Author unknown

Those that desire, but act not, breed pestilence.

William Blake

I shall tell you a great secret my friend. Do not wait for the last judgement, it takes place every day.

Albert Cairns

Fortune favours the bold.

Terence

When opportunity knocks, an entrepreneur is always home.

Victor Kiam

Footprints in the sands of time are not made by sitting down.

Proverb

Action is character.

F Scott Fitzgerald

Be not afraid of going slowly, be only afraid of standing still.

Chinese proverb

From where you sit, you can probably reach out and touch a life of serenity and peace. You can wait for things to happen and not be too sad if they don't. That's fine for some, but not for me. Serenity may be pleasant but it lacks the ecstasy of achievement.

Estée Lauder

The so called secrets of success won't work unless you do.

The author

An ounce of action is worth a ton of theory.

Frederick Engels

Wherever you see a successful business, someone once made a courageous decision.

Peter Drucker

Entrepreneurs don't sit around on their haunches waiting for something to happen, they make things happen.

Victor Kiam

We must use time as a tool, not as a couch.

John F Kennedy

What a day may bring, a day may take away.

Author unknown

Humans live far within their limits. They possess powers which they habitually fail to use.

Professor W James (Harvard)

The great aim of education is not knowledge but action.

Herbert Spencer

Acting is action. Action is doing. Find ways to do it, not to say it.

Stella Adler

A little knowledge that acts is worth infinitely more than much knowledge that is idle.

Khalil Gibran

Entrepreneurs' willingness to seize initiative sets them apart from their contemporaries.

Victor Kiam

You have to do something, anything, because YOU have to have control of your life.

Dr Phil McGraw

You learn a lot during teaching; however, seeing is not enough, you must do. Knowing is not enough, you must apply.

Bruce Lee

Do you want success, I mean really want success – to change your life and to really live? What's your answer – is it I think so? That's weak and indecisive. Is it no? That's game over and bin this book because it's a waste of your time reading it. Or is your answer yes? A timid and polite British style yes isn't going to be enough. Muhammad Ali was totally motivated, utterly psyched up to win, and he could yell – "I am going to win!" Have you ever noticed how positive the US athletes are before an event? They're interviewed and you hear them say with complete positivity and conviction, "I'm going out there to win!" Period. By contrast I've heard many British athletes saying, "Well I'm going to do my best so hopefully I'll be in the medals." It's in the British nature to be more reserved and polite. Nothing very wrong with that, but it doesn't give off the vibes of a powerful unrelenting attitude.

You need to take a deep breath, clench your fists and yell it out.......YES I CAN AND I WILL!! Now do it several times, each time forcing the energy to build.......feel it welling up inside you until it explodes.......because that's the power and drive you need to feel to succeed. It's a 100% belief in yourself. Total determination – it is an absolute and it's a prerequisite to action.

This is the wake up call – time to go to work.

Chapter 3

Supercharge Your Mind

Think of a battery. What makes it power the objects that it is put into? Energy. But to be more precise, positive energy. Positive thinking is one of the key ingredients for success and there is no success without it. Positive energy is positive thinking.

If you charge yourself up on negative energy (negative thought) then your mind becomes likened to a flat battery – it exists, but is, at that point in time, useless. GIGO, computer speak for Garbage In Garbage Out!

It seems that wherever and whenever someone comes up with a great idea and tries to do something positive, that well known group of people – the doom mongers, suddenly surface and go all out to tear the idea or proposed action to pieces as they embark on a fault finding mission. I cannot emphasise enough – if you have done your thorough research and planning and have the in depth knowledge of the product or service you are going to offer, do not listen to them! Their philosophy is one which breeds failure, destruction, and loss, even before the first step has been taken. I do of course generalise, but I think you get the point.

Ann Summers said, *"If you've got a good idea it's really important to stay focused and don't let the negative people put you off."*

Nothing will ever be attempted if all possible objections must first be overcome.

J R Simplot

I wake up every morning with the determination that this is going to be the best day of my life.

Richard Branson

I must win, I must always win, I cannot be number two.

Arnold Kopelson

To achieve great things, we must live as if we were never going to die.

Vauvenargues

There are always times when businessmen can make a good profit if only they could recognize and seize the moment, and if they could ignore the negative sentiments expressed by those who become prophets of doom.

John Paul Getty

The world belongs to the optimists. Pessimists are only spectators.

François Guizot

Poverty is attracted to the one whose mind is favourable to it, as money is attracted to the one whose mind is deliberately prepared to attract it, and through the same laws.

Napoleon Hill

It takes a certain kind of mind to see the beauty in a hamburger bun.

Ray Kroc

Love, work and knowledge are the well springs of our lives and they should also govern it.

Sean Connery

The mind is like a fertile garden. It will grow anything you wish to plant – beautiful flowers or weeds. And so it is with successful, healthy thoughts, or with negative ones that will, like weeds, strangle and crowd the others. Do not allow negative thoughts to enter your mind for they are the weeds that strangle your confidence.

Bruce Lee

As a man thinketh in his heart, so is he.

James Allen

Try to do just one positive thing each day toward your goal.

Anthony Robbins

Chapter 4

Goals are Greatness

Do you have a goal or goals? If the answer to this question is no, then stop where you are and think very carefully. If you don't know or are not certain then you will probably not succeed. You absolutely must have a goal, a target, call it what you will. I have asked many people what they want out of life, what ambitions, goals or dreams they have, what they want to achieve. I would say that 98% of those I questioned had such answers to offer as, "Well I wouldn't mind being rich," or "I want to be famous," or "I'd like to run my own business," etc. Others said, "I just want to be happy" or just "as long as I've got my health". All very commendable and pleasant to hear. But all of these are actually whimsical notions sometimes coming from people who believe in fairytales. The point was proven when I then asked them how they intended to achieve these 'goals'. I think only two or three people had a formulated plan or were actually doing something to reach specific goals and one ultimate chief aim in life.

So what is a clearly defined goal? Is it saying – I'd like to have a million pounds? No, it isn't. How about, I want to own a luxury overseas villa? No, that's not a goal either. A goal is: Five years from now, (write down a date) I will have banked £1 million.

That's a goal! It's specific. Now, how are you going to get there? That's the strategy part, the stepping stones, a series of smaller manageable goals leading to the ultimate goal. Each one of those stepping stones may require a business to be set up and as we have discussed, there is work to be done in each case.

I'll tell you about one of mine. I had a dream – I wanted to build a luxury villa overlooking the sea and the sunsets in an idyllic location on a Greek island. It wasn't until recent times that I finally set about actually doing something about it. I converted my dream into a specific goal. I set a time limit. Now here's the tricky bit – I wanted to achieve this without using any of my own money. This was partly because I had very little cash and partly because I was ambitious enough to see if it could be done. Lack of money was quite an obstacle.

I spoke to a few people, and despite them knowing what a determined fellow I am, they all doubted me, some even laughed and said it was a 'pie in the sky dream' that couldn't be achieved. They told me to get real. To me, my goal *was* real.

Despite not having the means to achieve any of this, I decided to travel out there and look at land. Within the first week, I had viewed several plots. The last one captivated me. The view was wow!

Now I had a goal that I didn't need to visualise any more – I could see it, and I really wanted it!

Raising the money to buy the land was yet another obstacle. They say the first money is always the hardest to raise. It became a goal. The solution was in family property – equity. Until recently the UK property market, carried prices that had been blown out of all sensible proportion – way beyond obscene and insane levels. In fact in 2009, at publication of this book, the prices are still far too high. The only advantage of that was that equity could be raised against it, and this is what many buyers raise their deposits on – equity in existing family property. They have no choice because their salary multiples won't come even close to allowing borrowing at the asking price level. The cost of my land wasn't far dissimilar to a first time buyer's deposit on a London flat. So therein I found the solution to that part of the problem. My father agreed to re-mortgage on the evidence of future value of the villa, and rental prospects, which by then I had thoroughly researched and had considerable knowledge of anyway, and knowledge and research are vital.

I knew the money to build the house would also have to be borrowed and I didn't own a property in the UK so there was no possibility of re-mortgaging on equity here. That was another obstacle and at this point it certainly seemed like a no win situation on face value. Fortunately I rarely take things at face value. So I still made it a goal to borrow money from a bank.

Then another obstacle surfaced. I couldn't borrow the amount I would need from a UK bank because very few of them will fund an overseas property purchase or build, even in Europe, which I think they should as we're all part of the same economic community. The few that would, set limits of 50-75% and there were more terms and conditions than words in the small print. That was unacceptable to me. I thought it was insane. Here you are proposing to build a villa, which upon completion, will be worth at least twice what it cost and it will become an eminently rentable commodity, yet banks in the UK are terrified at the prospect. They have so little vision. Okay, their loss!

The solution came when I discovered that banks in my chosen destination funded my type of project using entirely different lending criteria.

All these obstacles came about because of the difficult and perhaps unusual position I was in.

You will have obstacles as I did, no matter what you are doing. Life often deals them out in unfair portions. It really gets to you, but you have to fight it, I mean really fight it, sometimes until it nearly breaks you. I have been there many times. You simply must look upon those barriers as goals. Turn them into challenging goals to overcome and defeat and don't give up. A 'no' in one quarter is a 'yes' in another. The moral of this story is: Where there's a will there's always a way.

Here's a quick lesson that I learnt from a friend who has made millions – in fact he worked from the age of twenty eight until he was only thirty eight. I asked him straight. I said *"how did you do it?"* This is how the conversation went:

Peter: *"I sold microwave ovens."*

Me: *"But surely you can't make money from those unless you sell them to the masses."*

Peter: *"True, but I sold them when they first came into the country and they cost £2000 each...in other words, I sold them to the only people who could afford them: Rich people."*

Me: *"What happened then?"*

Peter: *"Well, the market changed. Microwaves became accessible to everyone and I wasn't in that market so that was the time to get out. I'd made quite a lot of money, so I bought some property and started renting it out. Then I went into selling conservatories."*

Me: *"But that's a killer of a game, the double glazing salesman, cold calling at people's doors. Surely there was no real money in that?"*

Peter: *"That's true also, unless you owned one of the big market leaders. I didn't, but that didn't matter because I wasn't selling the type of conservatories that you stick on the back of a three bed semi. I sold the kind that are twice as big as a three bed semi, the kind you attach to the back of very large detached country homes and mansions. Again I sold to rich people, only rich people, because they will always buy even when there's a recession, and that is the secret of my success."*

So I applied that advice to my circumstances and it didn't take much to work out that a private villa with a pool and stunning sea and sunset views on a Greek island is a luxury commodity that rich people would want to rent, but more importantly, could afford to rent!

What did I know about the travel business? Well, having been in it for thirteen years, quite a lot actually, but I'll come to that later.

In a recession, the average person who travels on holiday in the two and three star market has to cut back on luxuries. A holiday is one of the first luxuries to go for those people. However the wealthy are not affected by economic down turns in the same way as their less well off counterparts. Not only can they afford a holiday but they can afford a luxury holiday – a villa holiday no less.

People in the UK made massive profits in buy-to-let – if they bought in the late nineties. Now advisers are saying that if you get into buy-to-let, most areas are non-starters especially if you need 100% mortgaging because the cost may not be covered by the rent, even when the interest rates are low. With that in mind I'm building rather than buying. I don't think I need to spell out why. But if I choose, I could re-mortgage on the equity of the completed property and build more villas.

Now, just going back to my situation briefly, and here's the best part of all. Before construction had even started, three villa rental specialists were vying for contracts. So therein is yet another obstacle turned into a goal for which there is a solution – who funds the mortgage? Answer: The villa companies, indirectly. The mortgage on the land can also be funded out of the profit as are all the running costs. Sometime early on in the process I was watching a movie called 'Contact' with Jodie Foster. Hadden, played by the wonderful actor John Hurt said, *"Why build one, when you can have two at twice the price?"* I thought that was quite a good idea, but then I thought why borrow money for two? I adapted the concept, built one, and as I write these words, the second is going up for sale off plan, the profit from which clears the mortgage on the first, which I keep. Goal achieved! All this has led to another project built on experience in the travel business – a luxury villa rental business called greekislandvillas.net

It's no secret though – many people are doing it. I cannot give you investment advice because apparently the law doesn't allow it, but if you are in the fortunate position to have equity in a UK property, have you considered the overseas market? But there's a recession, and property prices have plummeted you say. Yes they have, but they will eventually go back up again. So if not now, later. You don't have to let a recession prevent you from improving your life. However, a warning; and I say this even as a pro-European, be very, very careful buying overseas. If you make a search in the UK it will need to be far deeper in some other countries. Get the very best advice you can from reputable agents and English speaking lawyers. Dissect the rental market in your chosen area with laser vision. Having said all this, my experience, and that of friends of mine, is that on average, in many overseas countries there are far better systems in place than in the UK, for example: no leasehold system in some countries. Also for the money you might need to buy a two bed terrace here, you can have a fabulous villa there!

It's vital you have an ultimate goal, no matter how many irons you eventually have in the fire. You must keep a focus on that goal. The irons in the fire should effectively be part of the overall plan with which you will achieve that ultimate goal. They are the stepping stones. With each step comes a small success. Each success brings you closer to realising your ultimate dream.

There is much advice given about concentrating on only one thing, one project or whatever. I would take issue with this, for if you are only involved in one project and have only one ball in the air so to speak, you risk bankruptcy (see chapter ten on diversification). You may lose many opportunities because all your time was spent on only one thing. If you are working a nine to five, five days a week, you have the evenings and weekends free. There is no excuse. You can utilise at least some of that time by working on an entrepreneurial venture. Use one of your lunch hours to visit a potential client or customer for example. So you lose a lunch hour, it won't kill you. Don't neglect your loved ones however. If you set an evening or so aside to work on your venture they should understand. After all, you simply want to create a better life for them. Perhaps you could find a way that they could be involved in your projects too.

Keeping a number of balls in the air is necessary. However, if you are sitting down to make calls related to a particular project, it's no good suddenly remembering a call you were supposed to make regarding a completely different project. Where possible, allocate a specific time period each day or week to each project. And don't sit around for days waiting for some potential investor or prospective client to call back, call the next one! A word of caution though – you are not superhuman so I would suggest that you do not begin with more than two or three projects, or better still, start with one that you can clearly visualise as something that can expand and develop. There's a fine line.

I'll say again – whatever you are doing, or want to do, you have got to have a clearly defined principal goal and at least an outline plan of how you are going to get there. After all what is the use of running if we are not on the right road.

To become a billionaire you have to have the mentality of a billionaire, a particular state of mind that concentrates all knowledge, energy and intelligence on the route toward a single unique and ultimate goal.

John Paul Getty

You have got to know where you are going to get there and nobody is going to get you there except you.

Joe Girard

The world stands aside for anyone who knows where they are going.

David Jordan

Singleness of purpose is one of the chief essentials for success in life, no matter what may be one's aim.
John Rockefeller

It's not enough to take steps that might one day lead to a goal. Each step should be a goal in itself whilst carrying you closer to your ultimate goal.
Goethe

You read a book from beginning to end. You run a business the opposite way. You start with the end, and then you do everything that you can to reach it. The beauty in setting a firm objective (starting with the end) is that the goal itself will begin to define what you must do in order to attain it.
Harold Geneen

I believe that language is the way to promote freedom and that words are the way in which we can all contribute to making a better world. That's why my ambition is to start up my own radical publishing company. Then I can do for books what I have done for cosmetics... make them high quality, affordable and available to everyone.
Anita Roddick

Most of us serve our ideals by fits and starts. The person who makes a success of living is one who sees his goal steadily and aims for it unswervingly. That's dedication.
Cecil B DeMille

This is a good example of what a goal is:

*My goal is simple. It is complete understanding of
the universe, why it's as it is and why it exists at all.*
Stephen Hawking

*When you are in the valley, keep your goal firmly in
view and you will get the renewed energy to
continue the climb.*
Denis Waitley

*You must have an aim, a vision, a goal. For the man
sailing through life with no destination or 'port-of-
call', every wind is the wrong wind.*
Tracy Brinkmann

Chapter 5

No Limits

There are literally millions of cases the world over, always have been and always will be, of people who have set out to achieve greatness despite painfully overwhelming odds against them. The seemingly impossible becomes reality. Go way back in history and you find the names of many.....

John Bunyan, Charles Dickens, Helen Keller, O.Henry, Robert Burns, Beethoven, and Milton and the list goes on, of great people whose lives were blighted by extreme poverty, illiteracy, imprisonment, dumbness, deafness and blindnes:

'I used to cry because I had no shoes, until in the street one day, I met a man who had no feet' – so what's your excuse?

What chance of success would you give a poor black woman born in the backwoods of Mississippi to a single teenage mother who was brought up in the inner city Milwaukee. She was raped at the age of 14 and gave birth to a son who died shortly afterwards. You might say not a cat's chance in hell, but not this lady – she's **Oprah Winfrey**. Her first job on radio was whilst she was in high school. She then moved over to daytime television and after her success boosting the ratings for a

Chicago TV show, she formed her own production company – Harpo.

The Oprah Winfrey Show is the highest rated show in television history and has boosted Oprah's value in to the billionaire status. She donates part of her money to various causes which benefit women children and families.

The bottomless pit of potential lurks within us all, in hidden talents and other skills. There are people out there with more raw talent in golf than Tiger Woods or any of the great names on the course today, greater actors than Robert De Niro or Meryl Streep, and potentially richer men and women than Bill Gates. But they will never realise this potential because they will never pick up a golf club, try to walk in front of a camera or get into action with any good idea they have.

But one of the key reasons such people and others will not reach great heights, is because they listen to and act upon the words of those who offer only discouragement – the 'know your limitations' folk. It's strange, but it always seems that such negative individuals are neither rich nor great achievers. They are THE BIG LIMITED PLC.

I like thinking big. To me it's very simple. If you're going to be thinking anyway, you might as well think big. Most people think small because they are afraid of success, afraid of making decisions, and that gives people like me a great advantage.

Donald Trump

My interest in life comes from setting myself huge, apparently unachievable challenges and trying to rise above them.

Richard Branson

Anyone can make £100 million, and I'm living proof of that.

Duncan Bannatyne

Better to get a stiff neck from aiming too high than a hunch back from aiming too low.

Jacques Chancel

Make no little plans; they have no magic to stir people's blood. Make big plans and aim high in hope and work.

Daniel H Burnham

The most absurd and reckless aspirations have sometimes led to the most extraordinary successes.

Vauvenargues

There are no limits to the mind except those we acknowledge.

Napoleon Hill

I was convinced that if you think small, you stay small, and I had no intention of staying small.

Ray Kroc

The significance of a person is not what they attain, but what they long to attain.

Author unknown

Hitch your wagon to a star. Let us not flag in paltry works which serve our pot and bag alone.

Emerson

At 74 I had sold my Kentucky Fried Chicken business for millions of dollars. I had started it at the age of 65.

Colonel Sanders

Make the most of what you have. I operated full time on that precept. If you can't have everything you think you deserve at that moment, then you would be best to surround yourself with symbols of your ideal. In that small office, I surrounded myself with images of the good life, the lovely and intricately tapestried life of my imagination, an imagination that has always been, I am proud to say, large enough to admit any possibility.

Estée Lauder

To be a movie star, you have to invent yourself.

Michael Caine

Look at all the people in the world who are unbelievably successful yet are dyslexic or have some other disability, all the great actors and business people. George Soros is dyslexic yet he's made over a billion dollars.

Anthony Robbins

Compared to what we ought to be, we are only half awake. We are making use of only a small part of our physical and mental resources.

Professor W James

If people cease to believe that they will become gods, they will surely become worms.

Henry Miller

Author's note:
I'd like to end this chapter by telling you a brief story. Whilst the events outlined in it were by no means brief they were never the less, moving.

It's the story of a little boy who was born in a French village that had been broken by war at the hands of the Nazis during the occupation. His family suffered numerous emotional traumas. They were plagued by problems with alcohol and were trapped in poverty. The young boy grew up with several serious speech impediments. He skipped school for a whole year and when he reached the age of thirteen he left school altogether.

He took a job at a printing firm but by the time he was fifteen he was hanging out in street gangs, many of whose members ended up in prison. There was no real help for him at home, not only due to the aforementioned problems, but also because, for example, his father was predominantly illiterate.

Today that little boy has been critically acclaimed as one of the world's greatest screen actors. He has starred in well over a hundred films. His name is Gérard Depardieu.

Chapter 6

Keep on Keeping on

Would you describe yourself as persistent? Edison made over 5000 attempts to produce the electric light bulb. He simply would not give in.

It's a very sad fact that most people pack up at the very first sign of rejection or failure and after only one shot at success. They are most of the way to nowhere. Others give up after only a few attempts. They are part of the way to somewhere. But not content with half measures, successful people utilise a number of essential ingredients and one of these is persistence, sheer persistence.

When I got no answers to my calls and letters, after a few months had passed I wrote again and said that I'd love to stop by and see him. Some more time passed to no avail so I wrote yet another letter suggesting a whole new way to make the deal. I was utterly relentless, even in the face of a complete lack of encouragement, because you know, much more often than you would think, sheer persistence is the only difference between success and failure.

Donald Trump

If successful people have one thing in common, it's this incredible perseverance.

Anthony Robbins

Is the door closed? Open another.

Victor Kiam

Vitality shows in not only the ability to persist, but also in the ability to start over.

F Scott Fitzgerald

Never, never, never, ever give up!

Winston Churchill

Besides the ability to write, I think you definitely need a thick skin, a survivability quotient. You've got to be able to bounce, because you're going to take a lot of blows. Your going to take blows from critics, you're going to take blows from people in the development business who tell you that your script is no good, that this won't work and that won't work, and you're going to have actors who tell you that it isn't going to work, and your going to have to make the movie over all these objections. You're going to have to be like a Sherman Tank and push your vision through. The secret is to keep going. I used to write scripts, two a year. I wouldn't take no for an answer. Agents wouldn't read them. I must have made a thousand letters of rejection in the seventies. I got used to rejection.

Oliver Stone

Sometimes crisis focuses the attention far better than when you are doing well. You re-evaluate your strengths and start again.

Richard Branson

I refuse failure and I never give up.

Regine

You are your first and best audience, long before anybody else hears you. So don't be an easy audience. Keep asking for more.

Michael Caine

Try harder every day for there will surely be tomorrows that will bring you a lot of satisfaction and a lot of money.

Thomas Watson Sr

Sure I am of this: you only have to endure to conquer. You only have to persevere to save yourselves.

Winston Churchill

The single most important route to success is persistence - never, ever give up!

Terry Matthews

Chapter 7

The F Word

A relative of mine was being interviewed following publication of his first novel. The interviewer asked him how he would handle his new found success. He replied: *"That's easy, just look at how well I handled failure."*

There is no greater buzz than transforming a temporary failure into an explosive success. Try it for yourself.

One of the quickest ways to total failure, by the way, is to go out and buy or produce huge amounts of stock with no orders. The Dragons' Den entrepreneurs are often telling people that they are taking a huge and dangerous risk by doing just that. Some of them even re-mortgaged their house to fund stock. There are exceptions to the rule of course, but not many. Stock for your own shop for example is different than stock to try and sell to some company. Sale or return is the golden rule for selling other people's products.

James Caan of Dragons' Den says, *"You can and you must learn from failure and we often learn more from our failures than from our successes. Entrepreneurs need to be prepared for things sometimes not working out as they had planned.*

They have to be ready to make sacrifices for the business and to take risks."

And **Doug Richard** says, *"If there is no risk, there cannot be reward. If it's not a risky opportunity then there's no reward of equal dimension. When people come to me and say, "I've got a risk free investment," the first thing I know is there's not much money to be made".*

If something was a loss, he wasn't really concerned with that; somebody else could clear that up. He was already on to the next thing. He wasn't reckless exactly, but he never stopped to consider whether that loss was too great and might hamper expansion. He just got on with expansion.
Jack Clayton (of Richard Branson)

Sometimes by losing a battle you find a new way to win.

Donald Trump

You can be discouraged by failure or you can learn from it. So go ahead and make mistakes. Make all you can because that's where you will find success, on the other side of failure.

Thomas Watson

Many of life's failures are people who did not realise how close they were to success when they gave up.
Thomas A Edison

A period of continuous bad luck is as improbable as always staying on the straight path of virtue. In both cases there will eventually be a curve.

Charlie Chaplin

The individual who is able to perceive even a glimmer of possibility in a situation that seems at first glance to be full of insurmountable obstacles is the one who is likely to reap the greatest benefits.

John Paul Getty

John Dryden wrote:
> *Fight on my merry men all*
> *I am a little wounded but I am not slain*
> *I will lay me down to bleed a while*
> *Then I will rise and fight with you again*

Don't be afraid of failure, you are never so close to victory.

Henry Ward Beecher

There is no success without hardship.

Sophocles

The world's entrepreneurs are divided into two categories – those that have failed repeatedly and those that are unknowns.

The author

The greatest glory is not in never failing, but in rising every time that you fall.

Confucius

Failure is only opportunity in work clothes.

Henry J Kaiser

We have all been failures, at least the best of us have been.

Jim Barrie

Entrepreneurs are those who understand that there is little real difference between obstacle and opportunity and are able to turn both to their advantage.

Victor Kiam

Ever tried, ever failed? No matter. Try again, fail again, fail better.

Samuel Beckett

For the entrepreneur, every rejection is only temporary. If you keep your eyes and ears open, today's failure can bring the opportunity to score more points tomorrow.

Victor Kiam

Poverty is the richest experience that can come to a person.

Edward Bok

Opportunity has the sly habit of sneaking in through the back door and it often comes disguised as misfortune or temporary defeat.

Napoleon Hill

Faced with a difficult situation, it is to himself that a man of character turns.

Charles de Gaulle

You're on the road to success when you realise that failure is merely a detour.

William Milnes Jr

Failures are like skinned knees; painful but superficial – they heal quickly.

H Ross Perot

If I fail, at least I will fail my way instead of somebody else's way.

Jodie Foster

It is not the critic who counts; not the man who points out how the strong man stumbles, or where the doer of deeds could have done them better. The credit belongs to the man who is actually in the arena, whose face is marred by dust and sweat and blood; who strives valiantly, because there is not effort without error and shortcoming; but who does actually strive to do the deeds; who knows the enthusiasms, the great devotions; who spends himself in a worthy cause, who at best, knows in the end the triumphs of high achievement, and who at worst if he fails, at least fails while daring greatly, so that his place shall never be with those cold and timid souls who know neither victory nor defeat.

Theodore Roosevelt

Show me the person who has never failed and I will show you someone who has never taken a risk. I'll show you someone who is not an entrepreneur.

Victor Kiam

When defeat comes, accept it as a signal that your plans are not sound, rebuild those plans, and set sail once more toward your coveted goal.

Napoleon Hill

Chapter 8

The Art of Persuasion Part 1

Robert Louis Stevenson said, *"We are all salesmen, we all live our lives each day by selling something."* Think about it. Selling does not necessarily have to be for financial gain, though that may well be the end result. You could be 'selling' your ideas to your husband or wife for certain home improvements (although I think you girls usually have the final say in such matters!). Maybe you are selling your ideas at a meeting, selling yourself at a job interview or selling your opinions in some way. I'm doing that right now, and I trust that if you are this far into the book, you have already bought it!

Teachers in schools for example, are sales people. You can liken the teacher to the sales person trying to sell the product or service which can be likened to the subject. In turn, the pupil can be likened to the prospective client or customer.

If you are a teacher let me ask you some questions: can you name the five popular bands followed by your pupils?. Can you name even one? Do any of your pupils come from another country? If so what do you know about it and their culture? What do you know about their families? What are your pupils' favourite pastimes? Do you address your pupils by their first names – I ask this because I think you should, but not if you expect them to address you as Sir or Miss or even Ma'am. I know I'm making a controversial statement here but I truly believe it's a fault in the system. Why should they respect you if you don't respect them? I have seen this in action, it works! Try it out for yourself. Want to persuade? Get in touch with the prospect's (or pupil's mind). You can't get them onto your level until you get onto theirs. It's called building subconscious rapport with the prospect.

There are no guaranteed sale clinching lines that you can learn from other people, though there are a myriad of sales training managers and executives who would have you believe otherwise. Similarly there are no objection-defeating lines to guarantee that you will, with their use, overcome any objections the prospect may raise. So do yourself a big favour, give the scripted sales lines, clichéd dialogue and cheap sales techniques a wide berth. They are painfully obvious and do not work, unless of course the prospect is completely gullible. The reality is that increasingly, today's clientele are a smarter breed. They will sense that scripted lines are not original and they are not your words. Quite possibly they will have heard them before so unless you are the next De Niro the sales lines will not come across as being from the heart. They'll seem unnatural because they are not, to put it simply, you.

Now I am not going to even attempt to teach you

how to sell because I don't believe anyone can do that. Though I have to say, I have met an unwelcome share of people claiming to be able to do just that. Great selling can often be achieved through change of attitude and approach. I think it helps if you have some natural ability, but it's not essential. You can however greatly improve any level of ability with a few simple tips. I will add to the words of the great persuaders listed below:

Develop your oratory skills even if it means taking elocution lessons. There's nothing wrong with that hard Glaswegian accent (I was born there, but I don't have the accent) but will it be understood the length and breadth of the country, or overseas for that matter? In the film *'My name is Joe'*, by the great director Ken Loach, they apparently had to add subtitles because filmgoers in the US couldn't understand what the actors were saying. Here's a thought – if you are going overseas on business, even on holiday, you should learn some of their language – it's damned disrespectful and arrogant to expect them to speak English. When they visit Britain do you speak their language?

Be yourself, be nice, be genuine, be interested in the client, be passionate about what you are selling, and saying. Believe me it comes across.

Get on first name terms ASAP. Right at the outset is always best. 'Mrs' is a title. Using it is not more respectful, why *do* people believe that it is? Let me tell you something about people – they have a great desire to be appreciated, wanted, needed and loved – informality and a one to one personal approach compliments those desires. Using 'Mrs', as in our example, only achieves two things: it tells you she is married and it tells you she is female and if you can't identify the latter, well, what can I say. I have never used titles, they're too formal. Your job is to make the prospect relax and to ensure you become their trusted friend. Selling successfully requires trust. Without it the prospect will not buy from you. Calling someone 'Mr' or 'Mrs' is actually a barrier, a small one at times I admit, but never the less a relevant one. Think about it. Start the conversation as though you know them, but be very careful - don't be too over familiar.

Only try to persuade a prospect to make a deal with something you genuinely believe in – something you would buy or have bought yourself.

John H Patterson said, "*Before you try to convince anyone else, be sure you are convinced, and if you cannot convince yourself, drop the subject.*"

Passion for what you are doing and selling is an incredibly powerful and influential tool but be warned, never try to fake it. Have you ever watched 'The X Factor' or 'American Idol' (ideas that made huge fortunes by the way)? How many times have you heard the entrants say "I'm so passionate about it"? Call me cynical but less than half the entrants who say that don't convince me. I hear the words but not the heart. It gets worse when they start crying and say "It means more than anything else in the world to me." Really? How can an eighteen year old who hasn't lived, been anywhere or done anything, say that? What about her family? So what's the point? Okay, the point is that for many of them the passion is for fame and fortune, not the music. If the only thing you want is to make millions for yourself so you can live the high life and become famous then I'm sorry but you need to take along hard look at yourself in the mirror. Actors and singers can become famous, but all of those I know didn't do it for money and fame, they did it for the art form, for escapism or other reasons – fame and fortune was a side effect of their being damned good at what they did, usually as a result of doing it differently. In the music and movie industry there is a constant and ever changing demand for something different, for new approaches and ideas that stand out.

Make sure you know what the prospective client needs and wants. They are two very different emotions that have to be specifically sold to. It could be argued that 'x' man or woman *wanted*, but didn't *need* a Rolex watch, because there are other good quality watches which had a lower price tag, or were arguably as good. That might be right, but the argument would be based on exactly that sort of line. What people fail to notice is that there is a mental need – in this example, the mental need is to feel good, to derive pleasure from that object, and what better way to derive pleasure from it than to own it. Establish the mental need, access it and sell to it.

How do you establish what that need is? Listen to people. How else can you find out what these needs and wants are, unless they tell you? Ask them and then listen to the answer – the key word here is *listen*. Don't waste your time trying to sell something that people don't necessarily need or want. There are too many Mickey Mouse outfits in that game.

Assuming that most of you, like me aren't high flying stock market traders making multi-million pound bonuses, then you might consider selling a product or service that either rich people want or non-rich people need. I think that's a fair analysis. The rich don't so much need as want, whereas people of modest means want also, but because of their financial status, the need of more important items becomes the priority. Behind this of course is the need for you to know who your target market is.

The employment pages of countless publications are full of ads promising vast sums of commission (and they are commission only), offered by companies claiming to be multi-million or even multi-billion dollar international organisations. Strange then is it not, that they only place a tiny ad, and stranger still is the fact that they often forget to mention the company name? On the rare occasions that they do provide their company name, you've never heard of them. The reality is that many of them are trying to sell unneeded and unwanted products or services. Don't get caught in this trap.

Maintain eye contact, always, including at the time you shake someone's hand, and when you do shake their hand remember, a weak handshake is like telling the other person you think they have a disease and that doesn't say much for your personality!

Smile when speaking. Richard Branson is a great role model – he has an infectious smile with nearly every word he utters. Confucius said, *"Man without smiling face must not open shop."* In modern terms that means people who don't smile shouldn't even be working in shops or any business where they come face to face with the public. And I tell you something else; have you ever noticed that you can tell when someone is smiling on the phone? Try smiling when you are on the phone, it has an incredible effect.

If you're an employer interviewing frontline staff, make certain they have the personalities that match the position before you worry about how pretty they are. You might think it's obvious but the current standard in Britain is very poor in that respect. Service with a smile will add huge value to your business. If you are that employer, remember that you should be smiling for your employees too. Smiling is a winning trait. Smiling sells and smiling persuades, it's not just your customers you have to persuade. There's many a company I have come across that doesn't really value its staff. **Richard Branson** said, *"The first rule of success in business is to look after your staff."* I would say that you could **adapt** and **apply** this to almost any situation ie, look after your client or prospective client!

Build rapport. Depending on the circumstances, I would spend hours spread over a number of days just getting to know my clients. Business should be the last thing on your mind. Look into psychology and the subconscious mind in relation to sales and communication skills and building subconscious rapport etc. This will also give you confidence and that impresses people. It's a natural thing to warm to a confident person. Confident people 'glow in the darkness', they radiate light and stand out in a crowd.

This bit is also relative to the chapter on knowledge: know your subject, don't bluff, it can be a catastrophic mistake.

Theo Paphitis of Dragons' Den says, *"Homework, homework, homework – make sure you know your subject. Make sure you have done your research. Make sure there is nothing anyone can tell you about your business (that you don't already know)."*

This is also very much applicable when you are starting out in business or a new business venture. Ensure that you have an in-depth knowledge of whatever it is you are going to do as a business venture.

If you really know your subject, but are still lacking a little in confidence then you can develop confidence, through books on the subject, and/or activities – physical types are good. Acting lessons are good too. The way I developed confidence was from some physical training, my acting profession and before that, from throwing myself in the deep end. Would you believe I actually became an overseas travel rep for Club 18-30! I can honestly tell you I was a complete introvert until that point and I quickly found that I had two choices – sink or swim. However, I am not afraid to admit that for a long time my confidence was just an act, a front. It was a performance, until it became second nature and part of me. Note that a lot of successful entrepreneurs are extroverts.

Above all, remember that you are also a 'product' and in many situations you will have to be marketed before you can market your wares.

Dress the part – it's no good wearing a three-piece business suit if you are selling holidays. Actors have to 'dress the part' in order to immerse themselves in the character, and certainly on screen and on stage, they will be wearing the clothes most associated with the character's occupation, life and personality. It is their job to convince the audience that they are the person that they are claiming to be. Actors are sales people! The analogy in this example is that the character is the product or service and the audience is the client.

In my opinion, and I speak from experience, suits and ties don't prove anything and don't always impress. Two very different examples from experience are estate agents, who often look (and sometimes act) more like lawyers, and tour operators' overseas reps – their clients are on holiday not at a bank meeting! A holiday is an informal event, so formal clothing just does not fit in, period. Why then are there travel reps walking around in 40 degrees of heat wearing suits and ties? There are two reasons, firstly because Britain, perhaps more than most other countries, has an obsessive preoccupation with uniform and formality and this is a very staid and dated trait. It is also because the overseas operations are often run by managers in the UK who know very little about people, yet ironically they tell their staff what to say to them and how to deal with them.

The suit is often as incredibly dull and boring as most of our sense of fashion in the UK. The suit never persuaded anyone of anything. Some would argue the 'professionalism' angle but I could easily disprove it. Don't be one of the thousand shades of grey suit people! There are those who believe that the formal grey suit image is what people want but more to the point, it's what they are being given, and therein are two very different things. If only people would try to give the prospect or client something different, and this applies to all aspects of your business. It doesn't mean you should wear ripped jeans and t-shirts though! If, after this, you still insist on wearing suits and ties at least buy from a decent tailor or better still go to an Italian retailer.

If you are a sales rep visiting clients at home, amongst your many thoughts should be the question, what might the clients be wearing when I visit them? Whatever it is, your best bet will be at the very least to lose the tie. Dress down to smart casual. Trust me on this, the clients will not have a problem with it. But it will have an effect. In this, or any sales environment, I would recommend that you adopt a strong personal and informal approach in all aspects of your contact with the prospect or client.

In the subconscious minds of the clients you will become one of them from the moment they lay eyes on you. What I am saying is that what you wear sends out a message that speaks to the prospect's subconscious mind in a subliminal way and says 'hey, he's like me', or 'he's one of us', and it does this the second they see you, before you even utter a word.

Why is it that car salesmen all have that same, well, car salesman look (as do estate agents), and employ that same car salesman talk? Have you ever been to a large car dealership? I took a trip to Mercedes-Benz World in Surrey – worth a trip, great building, great cars, but all the sales staff are wearing the same uniform completed by matching ties. I can't help noticing that there's this underlying corporate feeling in there and I find it a little unsettling. I mean who are they selling to? I see a lot of families and other members of the public, so I believe the uniform cloned look approach is less effective than a more smart casual and more individualistic look. It would be, at least visually, more friendly. Professionalism is about how efficient and knowledgeable you are so a suit may only enhance that in the right environment. A car surely is an object partly with a practical purpose, but it's also one that gives you pleasure – especially a new Mercedes. It therefore follows that buying it should be a fun experience and a frankly dull suit does not actually enhance the fun/pleasure element. Fun and pleasure should be injected into the process long before the client drives away in the new car. Even if only slightly, formal dress in most sales situations is a negative and incompatible element.

I was told a thousand times that I wasn't like all the other estate agents or all the other reps, that I was such a refreshing change. Observant people even pointed out my dress code as 'friendly'. My whole attitude and approach was different. But here's an important point I mentioned above – in estate agency, I made house-hunting fun. One company really didn't like that approach saying that this was a very serious business and large amounts of people's money was involved. My attitude was that firstly it was mostly a bank's money that was involved, but when it was the client's money that very fact should give them all the more reason to enjoy spending it – are you in property sales? Make the whole process of house hunting an exciting one and make it a challenge for yourself and the client whilst finding the property that <u>matches their personality and needs</u>. Find ways of using your personality and skills to take away the sombre from the process. People generally don't trust estate agents and that's understandable, but it's also a fixable problem.

If a client was in rented accommodation I sometimes went there to see what kind of place they rented (I'm talking about styles). I looked at their furniture. I played a kind of 'Through the Keyhole' game – you can imagine Lloyd Grossman saying, *"what kind of person lives in a house like this?"* Well I made it my job to find out. I match made people and properties. You could say it was a dating game of sorts.

I got a lot of viewings, sometimes 20-30 a day, to the point I had to delegate them out because I couldn't handle them all on my own. But here's a point of interest – I had those viewings and the property details hadn't even been printed. I used great verbal description – great words to paint a description of the property that got people so interested that they knew they had to see it. I described it with passion. The prospects became excited about being given the opportunity to be amongst the first to view. On a good day I created a frenzy of interest around a hot new property.

As it happens I very rarely, if ever, sent people sets of printed details but I used sell to serious buyers only. I wouldn't allow anyone to view a property who, if they had to sell to buy, hadn't at least received serious interest or offers on their property, or better still, who had reached exchange of contracts stage. If ever they protested I'd very gently ask them if they would like an estate agent to send people to their home who were not in a position to do something about it if they liked what they saw.

I would speak straight from the heart and I would point out that I didn't work with normal estate agency practices of putting people on mailing lists, then waiting two weeks to get sets of property details printed, and then sending piles of everything to them just because they were in their price range. This was because I had been on the receiving end of that myself, and it was a nuisance. I told them that the way I worked was very simple. If and when I found a property that matched their wish list, I was going call them to make an appointment to view it. All I asked them to do was to give me the benefit of the doubt and I promised them that in return I would not waste their time if the property didn't at least come very close to matching their criteria. Then I looked them straight in the eye with a smile and asked them to tell me everything they could about what they really wanted and needed. If it was feasible for their budget, I would give them my best effort to find it for them. Those were my terms and were my own words and I genuinely meant every one of them, so they worked. They were not sale clinching scripted lines, I had never been taught them. What they did was instil confidence and trust and that, as I have said, is a pre-requisite to selling. I was genuinely proactive in every sense of the word. I hear many estate agents saying they are proactive in their marketing and selling.

Here's a point about body language, actually relevant to so many professions – I intensely dislike talking to someone who stands behind a clipboard with it held against their chest all defensively as if they are afraid of something – it is very bad body language. (Read up on body language. Even the basics will do). If you use a clipboard, drop it down to the side of your hip or hold it in your hand out of the way. Most people don't notice the clipboard 'defence' consciously but their subconscious mind picks up on it immediately.

Just to qualify a couple of points. As an estate agent I broke the national sales record of a company that had around three hundred branches, and what's more I did it within my first five weeks, whilst still in training! The funny thing was, I had never been in that business before. In the travel business I spent thirteen summer seasons on a Greek island. People say that I hold what is statistically one of the highest excursion sales records for a single representative since mainstream tourism began in 1970 in that destination. Single-handedly, I grossed over 140K selling only three trips to clients from just one hotel on a Greek island in a four month period. Trust me that's a lot of excursions. I made money but I made a lot more money for other people. The good thing is they never forgot it.

I had however, negotiated a unique self-employed commission-only deal. It gave me a huge incentive and the freedom to make decisions and run the show in my own style. The tour operator also got an 80% reduction in complaints from the previous year and significant repeat business thrown in. During my time in that business I also created a new excursion on the island which was the most successful ever, with an average 95% booking rate. I could give you the details of it but that would be consultancy and then I would have to charge you!

I sold three things in the travel business apart from excursions. I'm sure you know what they were – I sold myself, I made things easier for people (I sold simplicity), and to some extent I sold solutions – the solutions to help the client's goal of having a more fulfilling holiday and therefore a more successful one. But don't forget that I really believed in what I was selling and saying.

If you haven't sold something on the phone, then after the prospect initially sees you, it is the spoken word that ultimately convinces. All the greatest ideas in the world would never have become anything more than impulses of thought had the spoken word not been used. It is by far the most powerful medium for conveyance of great thought and the means through which those ideas are converted into money. It's true that it is the person underneath the clothes and what they say that counts in the end, but why be underneath the wrong clothes? The right clothes can give you that edge of maybe only a few percent but that could be just the difference you need.

I don't know the rules of grammar. If you're trying to persuade people to do something, or buy something, it seems to me you should use their language.

David Ogilvy

Man without smiling face must not open shop.

Confucius

He who wants to persuade should put his case, not in the right argument, but in the right word. The power of sound has always been greater than the power of sense.

Joseph Conrad

If I'm say, launching a financial services company, I won't use words like 'bid' 'offer' 'spread', I will use language that people understand because that's the language I understand.

Richard Branson

Your smile will give you a positive countenance that will make people feel comfortable around you.

Les Brown

I always look each person squarely in the eyes, and whenever possible, try to say something personal. It might only be a small compliment but I give each person my undivided attention and I don't allow anything to distract me. Each person whose hand I shake is the most important person in the world to me at that moment.

Mary Kay Ash

You usually discover that if you make things easier for people, you gain their sympathy.

Aristotle Onassis

You can't sell anything you wouldn't buy yourself.

Victor Kiam

Most people try to take the horse to water and make it drink. Your job is to make the horse thirsty.
Gabriel M Siegel

Keep a tan all year round, even if you have to use a lamp. To most people a tan in winter means only that you have been where the sun is and in that respect, sun is money. Live in an elegant building, even if you have to take a room in the attic. You will rub shoulders with wealthy successful people in the corridors and elevators. Frequent luxury cafes, even if you have to sip your drink....
Aristotle Onassis

Never leave your details, your name and number more than once because it makes you look desperate.
Richard Branson

Change your whole attitude from one of trying to be interesting to one of trying to be interested.
Jay Abraham

Would you persuade; speak of interest, not of reason.
Benjamin Franklin

If there is one secret of success, it lies in the ability to get other people's points of view and see things from their angle as well as your own.
Henry Ford

If you want to gather honey, don't kick over the beehive.

Dale Carnegie

When I sold somebody a car, I told them they were buying two things; they bought a beautiful car and they bought Joe Girard.

Joe Girard

I consider my ability to arouse enthusiasm among people to be my greatest asset. And the way to develop the best that there is in a person is by appreciation and encouragement.

Charles Schwab

No matter what the reason, if you start screaming and shouting, you look like a fool and you earn the disrespect of everyone.

Michael Caine

I can live for two months on a good compliment.

Mark Twain

One of the best ways to persuade others is with your ears – by listening to them.

Dean Rush

What really flatters someone is that you think them worthy of flattery.

George Bernard Shaw

A few laughs go a long way to making a potential client comfortable.

Victor Kiam

It's an old maxim that a drop of honey catches more flies than a gallon of gall. So it is with people: if you would win them to your cause, first convince them that you are their sincere friend. Therein is a drop of honey that catches the heart, which, say what you will, is the great high road to their reason.

Abraham Lincoln

I am hearty in my approbation and lavish in my praise.

Charles Schwab

The deepest principal in the human nature is the craving to be appreciated.

William James

Silence is golden. The more you listen, the more obligated people become to you.

Jo Girard

I made him an offer he couldn't refuse.

Mario Puzo

K.I.S.S. – Keep It Simple Stupid.

Various

Chapter 9

The Art of Persuasion Part 2
Business is Business

There are of course countless types of businesses globally, varying in size from the one person working from home, to the international empire employing tens of thousands of people. The principles of business however, are pretty much the same across the board. They begin with an idea as I discussed in chapter one, action is then taken upon the idea, and somewhere down the line a product or service is sold at a profit.

Now and again someone crawls out of the woodwork and runs against the grain of the business establishment – the men in grey suits. I have highlighted some entrepreneurs whose names I will use again as examples – Richard Branson and Anita Roddick. You can't help but love them, and their approach. If you are going to be inspired by someone, they are as worthy contenders as anyone. Inspiration is a great thing, so be inspired, but don't copy.

I am not a big businessman. I am just a person engaged in a number of creative projects and businesses that give me pleasure. I have always wondered though, by what scale can you call a business big? To me a business is big when it takes up all of one's time. It does not have to be a multi-million pound company to be big. Business is business.

I follow two simple rules for involvement in any project, including this book: I keep it simple and I keep it fun. I simply will not get involved in something I don't enjoy.

I'd like to talk about various things one can do to make a business more appealing to the prospective client and therefore more successful. I won't talk about stocks and shares, complex economic structures or taxation because frankly I know very little about these subjects, and I have even less desire to understand them.

In my opinion, a very worthwhile practice which you could form into a habit and perfect, is the art of what I call 'projection'. That is to say where you appear to head a larger business than you actually do. Actually, many small businesses try to achieve this but fail. Usually this is because they lack the skills to market and present a powerful image. Think of the cinema for a moment. The image in the lens of the projector can be likened to you and your small business. If you wish to present a larger picture then it is your job to become the image on the screen – the image that the public see. Many people actually 'project' themselves even on their resumes, by exaggerating their achievements and some by 'dressing up' the wording used to describe those achievements. There is a marked difference between the two. Projection is quite justified depending of course upon the image you wish to present. Lying about your company size and achievements however will get you caught out and then your credibility has gone. But be warned, some companies and individuals will run checks into your company before engaging you. If you claim your business is worth millions, but in reality, it is run from your kitchen table an hour a day after work with a turnover of £200 a week, you will probably fail to get the contract. (Having said this there are stories of people who run even multi-million pound businesses from their kitchen tables. It depends what business you are in). Chances are, the people that may have hired your services, will know others in the same type of business and may well talk about you. Then you will find your name is dirt. The bottom line is found in the old saying – honesty is the best policy. So project, honestly.

There are many ways of achieving this from simple use of words like 'we' instead of 'I' and phrases like 'It's <u>our</u> company's policy to deliver the most competitive prices in the market.'

With these concepts and many more besides, you are appearing to be bigger than a one man or woman business without actually stating that you are.

Company stationery and some form of marketing and advertising is essential if you are offering a product or service.

I can't emphasise enough that you must get your image right and develop your own unique style; one suited to your product or service. Change your name if necessary, develop a punchy, catchy company name – there is enormous power in a good name.

Why do you think actors change their names? Remember Michael Caine's words, *"to become a movie star you have to invent yourself,"* (he used to be Maurice Micklewhite).

Names, Logos and Slogans
You've heard the saying *'it's all in the name'*. Well actually a lot of it is. The right name for your business is vitally important. I believe it can attract or repel a prospective client.

The right name can sell a product or service on its own. I think that building brand names is a lot easier with a great name. How you come up with it is a different matter. You can pay someone to think one up – I've done it for a few people. You can break down the problem. The company name is pretty much the first thing the customer hears of or sees, so if it grabs them, all the better. With few exceptions such as those where big brands have been developed like the RAC, ICI or BP (originally marketed in their longer versions), random letters like these should be avoided as they are impersonal and don't tell the prospect anything.

Using a name that describes (albeit very briefly) what you do or where you are is sometimes an advantage as it can imply longer term establishment and pride in a local area or town. My only issue with this is that it's a bit of a common practice. More importantly, perhaps when you come to expand to a larger geographical area, it can be restrictive.

It can be a strong sign of trustworthiness and longevity if you are willing to use your own name as a business. It helps though to have a good flowing name or perhaps an unusual or striking one. If you don't, then consider changing or altering it.

High alphabetical order may be important in a telephone directory but on an internet search it may have little use and this is also the case for a high street retail store.

Stay away from those corny sounding clichéd slogans – on hairdressers, for example, I have seen 'A Cut Above the Rest', and many companies use the slogan 'You've tried the rest now try the best'. Such slogans are common and make you look small, cheap and unimaginative. Inject some class!

Taste and style are commodities that people desire.

A slogan I came up with for a new airline in development was '*An Air of Difference*'. I got involved in marketing a removals business, and simply came up with '*A Great Move*'. When I was at college I came up with a slogan for a new aftershave. The ad campaign for the product had to tie in with the Olympic Games. I came up with the slogan '*For Winners Only*' and I designed an ad with a bottle of the aftershave standing on the gold medal platform with a gold medal around the neck. One of the college tutors decided the idea was so good he took the idea to the manufacturer. The only problem was that he didn't ask for my permission and he didn't tell me what he was doing. One day I saw some of my ideas on television but I had moved to Greece by that time so didn't discover it until it was too late. I was young and naïve. Always protect your ideas!! Although I spent three years at college studying creative advertising and marketing, and that gives me some advantages, I really believe that if you put your mind to it you can come up with a great name or slogan too. If you're struggling, then contact me and we can work something out.

Websites
When you develop a website, and you absolutely should, put together several email addresses for different departments, so that it seems there are at least several people working for the company, even

if there isn't. As an example, you might come up with 'enquiries@halcyonindustries.com'. If there are several people involved in your project they should all have individual email addresses with their names on them anyway.

One of the most important but commonly omitted elements of so many websites is a telephone number. It's infuriating that so many companies are seemingly impossible to contact by phone, because for love nor money you can't find their telephone number on the website. You click on contact and there's still no number, just questions, and sometimes not even an email address! This annoys people because it's in our nature as a species to prefer personal contact – we want to speak with someone. Don't get into that practice. I'll tell you the only company that I have bought from which doesn't seem to have a telephone number on their website and that's EasyJet, but I did find a normal landline number for them!!

Websites are a perfect example of the application of the KISS plan. Keep the website simple – uncluttered. The layout, colour schemes and typefaces will depend heavily on what you are selling. In creative advertising design you learn not to mix contrasting typefaces. Variations of Helvetica and Arial typefaces are similar and are clean and contemporary.

Some websites have little or no images on them. I think this is a big mistake. Most people are drawn to visual images – pictures sell, but they need to be good. So many companies have such awful photography. For example, most estate agents have terrible pictures of the properties they are marketing. They don't realise the importance of great shots – always a dull wonky shot of some dull looking property often taken on a dull day. Most houses have at least one room or part of one which, with a great shot, could help sell the property. Clever agents would use a great shot of that room as the feature shot instead of an exterior shot. On the rare occasions that I sent details out, I sold real estate with great shots – it works! In all media advertising the photography needs to be great. I know you will say, "it's easy for you to say, you have had your photography published". And to that I would respond by saying, "who said you had to take the pictures?" Find someone who can – it doesn't have to cost the earth. Chances are you might know someone who has a talent for photography. Avoid clichéd shots though. If you really want advice or help with things like website design, advertising concepts and ad design, photography or even corporate DVDs or television commercial production, then contact me – details are on the last page. I know quite a lot about these subjects but if it's something I can't help you with then I know many wonderful and talented people in those fields who can.

Telephones

Avoid 0870 and even 0845 numbers. Many people have call inclusive contracts on their home phones so that they can call land line numbers at no extra cost. When you call an 0870 number it's quite expensive. Many companies seem to forget that people have mobile phones and calling 0870 numbers from them costs the earth. They also forget that 0800 numbers are only free from landlines. It all gets worse when you are left in an automated queuing system for ages before you eventually get connected to some puppet on the other side of the world, sitting in a call centre, reading from a script. Want to persuade? Avoid the above practices and offer great service. Call centres by the way may save big companies money but being put through to one is quite possibly one of the most annoying and frustrating experiences a customer can have. Most companies know this but do little or nothing about it because the complaints, even though sometimes in the tens of thousands, are outweighed by larger profits and the need to satisfy shareholders.

I'd like to talk about business premises especially, but not exclusively, shops because I feel this is often a poorly thought out area, despite there being many aspects of it that are incredibly important in relation to persuasion and sales. I could simply say that you know as well as I do that there are many shops that you find pleasant shopping environments and just as many that are not so pleasant and leave it at that, but I feel some further analysis and thought on this subject is necessary.

Firstly I commend anyone who runs a business from home because boy, are they keeping costs down and saving money. Similarly if you have an internet based business you have the potential to make great cost savings which of course, in turn, can allow you to offer better value to your customers.

On this subject **Theo Pahitis** says, *"The retail environment is currently changing rapidly. This is partially because of the internet, which has opened up a huge world at the touch of a button. Selling on the internet means that you don't have to pay high-street rents and employ lots of assistants. You can also trade on eBay. You could simply have a lock-up and keep all your products there. It's really fantastic – everyone can become a shopkeeper. The amount of business being carried out on the internet now is shifting the balance of power. The internet has unshackled the business world."*

However, there's a lot to be said for being able to walk into a store, to see, feel and try on or test a product. So if your business really needs a premises then very careful thought needs to go into it.

Factors that will affect sales up or down are:

Location

How visible is the store? Is it in a position busy with pedestrians or a place where people just drive past? If it's drive past, does it have parking? How many Halfords' stores have you seen that don't have parking? Is it a business that someone would expect to find in that location? I say this because if it isn't, it could be turned to an advantage – going against the grain!

Shop Frontage

In addition to the name, I would consider adding a slogan to a shop front and a telephone number and if it doesn't clutter the aesthetic, I might even add the website address because people may not always have time to call in. If the company name is strong enough people will remember it even if they only glanced, then they can look it up on the internet. I would also do something that most shops in every high street seem to lack to the frustration of many shoppers – the street number!

Opening Times

Most people work 9-5. Often the only chance they get to shop for things other than food is during a lunch break, a time when they would probably prefer to be eating and relaxing. Another opportunity is most likely to be on a Saturday. Major supermarkets open late into the evenings (some are even 24 hours) and at weekends too. Look how busy they get at those times, even on a

Sunday. Learn from this. Do you see those Indian corner shops closing at 5pm either? People often wonder how it is that many of our Asian people are so successful. I would say it's because they work harder, longer hours than most white Europeans and they also involve their families in their businesses. This doesn't mean you have to personally put in a 15 hour day. It would probably be a major advantage to you to run an additional online side to your retail business – one with a payment system attached. It could be generating sales orders while you are at home relaxing.

Colour

This is so important – how many business premises have we seen that have awful colour schemes? Think warm, think friendly, think calming – neutral colours. Use the colours to make products stand out. Depending on the business type however eg, a trendy record/music store, you may want to use colours more associated with that business. But always keep in mind your target audience – age group, social sector etc. People associate certain colours with particular social levels eg, the Racing Green and gold of Harrods are a blend associated with upmarket products and services sometimes found in older and long established traditional companies. I love those pastel rustic colours found on shutters and doors of properties in the Provence region of France and I've noticed that they are used increasingly in a growing number of independent stores selling the individualistic French style rustic household furnishings. You find those stores mostly in fairly affluent market towns.

Lighting

I have a big issue with this. Strip lighting should be outright banned, at least the old type should be – it's so stark and cold. Lighting can make all the difference to whether or not a person wants to stay in a place. I'll use the movie analogy because it's relevant – lighting is used to create depth of field and to make an actor look great and also for other technical reasons, but primarily it is used to create mood. The variations are endless. Too much lighting kills a scene so think about creating mood with the lighting. Often, less is more!

Layout

Ease of access and ease of finding things are also vitally important. How many times have you had to ask where something is in a shop. In some stores like supermarkets it's a common problem but I'm not sure they can do much more than they do already to make it easier.

Music

Again, very important. A good DJ will play music to suit his audience. Use it only if relevant and choose carefully. If you must employ a teenage girl in a shop that mainly sells to the elderly in a sleepy retirement coastal village you won't do yourself any favours if she has access to the CD player or is allowed to bring in her iPod and speakers.

Staff

Employ smiling faces with warm and genuine personalities who communicate clearly and are enthusiastic. Don't employ people on the grounds that they are beautiful. There are many people I have noticed working in UK shops, mostly female actually, who are more often than not from certain countries that shall be nameless, who look great, but it is commonly said of them that they don't smile. Usually they are lovely when you get to know them, but something in their nature makes them hesitant to smile up front and that is very dangerous for a business. Now I know that this is the sort of subject that causes national debates about political correctness but PC is a pain in the proverbial backside.

Let's look at the restaurant business for a moment. I am, perhaps for obvious reasons, more than a little biased towards Greek food. I also love Italian and French as well as many others (sorry not a fan of UK cuisine). Now I'm the very opposite of racist but please, if you are setting up a French restaurant, it's a bit if a con if you market it as French when you only have some dishes with French sounding names but have a Polish chef, Slovakian waitresses and a South African barman. If I were launching a restaurant of a particular flag, I would fill it with staff from that country especially the chef, and what's more I'd make sure the public knew it because offering authentic cuisine cooked by a chef from that country is something people really want but rarely find. I don't understand why, but the major chains can't or perhaps don't want to give the public the real thing. I would make the entire experience authentically French, Italian, Greek or English, or whatever the theme was. I'm telling you it's a very effective tool. I've seen it in practice.

Now I'm going to mention age. Personally if I was buying a property for example, I would not be happy dealing with a 20 year old who still lives with his parents. Why? Because what does he know about property and moving when he has never experienced it himself? Most people who have moved a few times have had at least one bad experience and many people find it traumatic. I was always able to smooth that worry out because I had experienced the same problems in the past so I could understand the clients' concerns and we could relate to each other. So, controversially perhaps, what I'm saying is that 'age discrimination' is actually justified in some circumstances because with age comes life experience and in my view that has a greater underlying value.

Above all else, in a sales environment, your staff are there to persuade for the benefit of the customer, themselves and you. If you don't look after them they won't look after you or your business. They need to be motivated and to feel good about themselves and about their value to you and your company, and guess what, it's down to you to build all that into them and to get the best out of them. Give praise and give it lavishly and use every genuine means at your disposal to make them feel great and an integral part of something special. Then, when you are ready to expand your chain, those amazingly talented people you have helped develop, may just be the very people to run your next branch and the thought of that possibility, may, in itself be a great incentive for them. Your staff are the most important part of your company. If you don't agree with that, time to close up shop and do something else. I can tell you, there are many companies who clearly don't believe in that and they have a generally unhappy workforce and a staff turnover to match through resignations that will eventually cripple them.

When **Theo Paphitis** buys a business he gets all the staff together and asks them who is the most important person in the company. Invariably they say the customer. Wrong, he says. Then they point to him. Wrong again he says, and he points to them. They are the most important people in the business. Obviously when you are dealing with a client they are the most important person at that time.

For the benefit of employer and prospective employees, I'll repeat something I said earlier:
'*The principles of sales and negotiation transcend all business and the only real variable is the product or service. Product knowledge can be gained by*

almost anyone provided they are interested in it. In other words actual advanced detailed product knowledge should not be a pre-requisite to gaining employment in a field the candidate is really keen on and interested in."

I'm going to add another thought for employers and sales employees. Structured commissions eg, 5% if you reach X, 10% if you reach Y and 15% if you reach Z, OTE (on target earnings) are not an incentive – they're very unfair terms that are heavily biased in favour of the company to make *them* more money. A generous fixed commission rate is a far greater incentive and rightly so. It's simple to use and simple to work out. A sales person should never have to spend a lot of time scaling some complex structure to work out what they have earned that week.

Also, I would say that some incentive gifts are also dubious in value and they don't pay the mortgage. The gifts should be a generous additional surprise or simply given to the top sales person that week or month.

Another problem I've seen which turned up in estate agency was that some companies would get the negotiator to go out and find properties, then contract them, write up all the descriptions, do the floor plans (often on complex and time consuming computer programmes), and then photograph the property (often badly). I sometimes saw people doing that several times a week – what time did they have left to do the selling? Not a lot. Bad practice. If a sales person concentrates on selling, it leads to more sales and that's good for everyone. I think you get the point but to give you an analogy, the police will tell you that they ought to spend a lot less time filling out forms and a lot more time on the streets catching criminals. In this point the conclusion is: sales/persuasion is also about good time management, so a company should think about that before overloading its sales force with too many other duties that could be carried out by someone else.

James Caan says, "*Adopt a win win attitude....to really succeed long term you need to make sure that the people around you win too.*"

Company Vehicles
Company vehicles are a great opportunity to advertise your product or service with your livery emblazoned along the sides and back. The colour of the vehicles should match the company brand colour scheme. (Hopefully you won't have chosen colours like brown or banana yellow!).

How many times have you seen a company vehicle, especially a van or truck, which is covered in dirt? Sometimes it's even a vehicle carrying food! If your company vehicle is filthy, it doesn't matter how great or famous your company name is, because I can assure you, the dirt on your vehicles won't help enhance your company image.

Unfortunately, many of the drivers have no respect for the vehicle because it isn't theirs. The interiors are often a pigsty and it makes you wonder what kind of conditions these people live in at home. As for the driving standards of some, the word maniac comes to mind and that isn't good advertising either.

Unless your company vehicles operate in a quarry, there's no excuse. They should be kept immaculately clean and it should be the driver's responsibility to either keep the vehicle clean or to arrange to have it cleaned, even if that driver is you. In Germany I met the owners of a company employing 50 people. They were mucking in to clean vehicles with their staff and they did it once a week, every week! That is also good motivation and even better leadership!

The first rule of success in business is to look after your staff.

Richard Branson

Your people are your business.

James Caan

It never stops and I would not have it any other way. I try to learn from the past, but I plan for the future by focusing exclusively on the present. That's where the fun is, and if it can't be fun, what's the point?

Donald Trump

People think I'm a gambler. I've never gambled in my life. To me a gambler is someone who plays slot machines. I prefer to own slot machines. It's very good business being the house.

Donald Trump

Knowing your strengths, you can see where they will lead you.

Victor Kiam

I am convinced that the more money a new business needs to begin with, the less chance it has of being a success.

Mark McCormack

The worst thing you can possibly do in a deal, is to seem desperate to make it. That makes the other guy smell blood and then you're dead. The best thing you can do is deal from strength, and leverage is the best strength you have. Leverage is having something the other guy wants, or better still needs, or best of all, simply can't do without.

Donald Trump

Be wiser than other people if you can, but do not tell them so.

Lord Chesterfield

You must cut your loss makers because they will drain the company and ultimately bankrupt it.

Richard Branson

To get results, stimulate competition. Not the sordid competition based only on gain, but rather more noble emulation; that of the desire to do better. To surpass others and to surpass oneself.

Charles Schwab

Business? It's quite simple – it's other people's money.

Alexander Dumas

In selling, treat relationships as if they were precious gems.

Victor Kiam

To my mind, the best investment a person starting out in business could possibly make is to give all their energies to work, just plain hard work.

Charles Schwab

Adopt a win win attitude....to really succeed long term you need to make sure that the people around you win too.

James Caan

In business, keep the small talk small – it has no place in business. You might win the debate but lose the order.

Victor Kiam

I will speak ill of no one and speak all the good I know of everybody.

Benjamin Franklin

I would never cheat anyone, and I expect that from others. It's very unpleasant to discover otherwise. Paramount is about the only company I haven't sued.

Sean Connery

You always have to replenish the well where you get your water, otherwise it will run dry.

Steven Spielberg

If you have to be in a soap opera, try not to get the worst role.

Boy George

To be successful, you've got to grow and you've got to contribute beyond yourself.

Anthony Robbins

Take care of the down side and the upside will take care of itself.

Donald Trump

The business of America is business.

Calvin Coolidge

Remington was raising its prices to keep pace with the competition. This was not just unsound fiscal policy, but a public relations disaster. Remington was made to look like a follower not a leader.

Victor Kiam

My formula for success? – Rise early, work late, strike oil.

John Paul Getty

If you want to send a message, try Western Union.

Sam Goldwyn
(remark directed at the Art House movie makers and use of non commercial genres to make statements)

Be everywhere, do everything and never miss an opportunity to astonish a client.

Margaret Getchell

Early to bed, early to rise, work like hell and organise.

Al Gore

Entrepreneurs must avoid getting too involved with products that are copies of whatever is currently hot with consumers. You have to ask yourself – what is the products USP: Unique Selling Position. What makes it stand out against the competition ie, better build, comparable, quality, lower price etc, etc.

Victor Kiam

Invest in inflation, it's the only thing going up.
Will Rogers

Stay flexible, never get too attached to one deal or approach. Keep a lot of balls in the air, because most deals fall through, irrespective of how promising they first seem. Once you have made a deal, create at least half a dozen angles to make it work.
Donald Trump

Pan Am takes good care of you, Marks and Spencer loves you and Securicor Cares. At Amstrad, we want your money!
Alan Sugar

If you pay peanuts, you get monkeys.
James Goldsmith

Chapter 10

The Big Split – Diversification

You have no doubt heard the saying about not putting all your eggs in one basket. There is great wisdom in these words that any business would do well to note carefully and preferably at the outset. It was with this in mind that I had to learn a very hard lesson in the recession at the beginning of the early '90s.

Observe if you will, a common denominator in thousands of businesses that have collapsed, particularly, but not exclusively, during recessions. They concentrated most or all of their efforts in a solitary service or product.

Now this is, of course, not a claim that lack of diversification is the sole cause of all business closures but it strikes me that in many cases it's at the top of the list. Perhaps they just could not compete in the market, or there were other problems within the structure, such as in the case of Woolworths. I would add that in their case I personally think that for many years they had a very dull and dated image. They left the refitting and modernising of their stores too late and they also seemed to lose their identity – question: what did we go to Woolworths for?

The bottom line with all this, is that times change, and with changing times, come new trends, fads, fashions, call them what you will – demand rises and demand falls. It's frustrating sometimes to hear that this or that company has just folded with the loss of so many jobs. The company made carpets or wallpaper or whatever, and one has to ask amongst other questions – is that all they did?

The CEO of Sainsbury's recently pointed out that one of the main reasons they are doing so well in recession (and creating several thousand new jobs in the process), is because they sell food and people always need food. Supermarkets of course sell a huge and diverse range of food and other products!

If you were investing in stocks and shares, would you place the money you have with one company? Of course not. You invest in a number of different company's shares to spread the risk. You don't have to be a stockbroker to work that out.

Here's a short rhyming story and I make no apologies for it. I use it only as an example, but it is of the utmost importance. Do you remember the occasions when Britain's farming industry was hit by disease in various live stock?

There once was a farmer whose business was pigs, and it was only pigs that paid for his digs. Then one day the pigs got diseased and the farmer's business suddenly ceased.

It's not funny is it? The rhyme was made up by a farmer whom I was fortunate enough to meet. He told me that he had put everything he had into the business, all his eggs in one basket. My response was, "but you don't deal in eggs do you, only meat?" You can't predict the future when you only do one thing. Let me rephrase that; you can't *afford* to predict the future when you only do one thing. And when it all goes wrong, for whatever reason, the winners will be the ones who can pick themselves up out of the mess – they will be in the minority. The losers will be those who will look for someone else to blame. They will be in the majority.

A company must produce several different products so that when the demand goes down for one or two, the company can deploy its assets to the products for which there is demand.

Harold Geneen

It's nice to build a successful hotel but it's a lot better to build a hotel attached to a huge casino that will earn you fifty times what you would ever make renting rooms.

Donald Trump

In business, the important thing is to adapt and to be sufficiently diversified so that a single mistake does not compromise your entire future.

An Wang

Mr Getty is in a rich man's business. He produces oil and he carries it. All I do is carry it.

Aristotle Onassis

Continuous improvement and continuous change are the hallmarks of our business.

David Sainsbury

We must become cool again.

Herbert Hainer

(Chairman of Adidas on rebranding effort)

To improve is to change. To be perfect is to change often.

Winston Churchill

We can no longer let the threat of an early frost send a chill of fear throughout a large portion of our workforce. Diversification is the only answer.

Alan Autry

Chapter 11

Leader of the Pack

So you want to be a leader of others? Fine, but first you must learn to give others something to follow. There's no escaping the facts. People can only be led by those who inspire them, who give them more than just a sense of worth, but make them feel great. I would say that Richard Branson is one of the grand masters of that art.

Get people involved in your exciting projects. Their efforts must be highly valued, and when success comes, you must reward them handsomely. Words of praise alone or a pat on the back won't do. These gestures don't pay the rent, but they should be used at every opportunity.

Keep away from people who try to belittle your ambitions. Small people always do that. The really great make you feel that you too can become great.
Mark Twain

A leader must take people from where they are to where they have never been before.
Henry Kissinger

I believe in benevolent dictatorship provided I am the dictator.

Richard Branson

The heights by great men reached and kept,
were not attained by sudden flight
but they, while their companions slept,
were toiling upward in the night.

H W Longfellow

The true leader always keeps an element of surprise
up his sleeve which others cannot grasp, but which
keeps his public excited and breathless.

Charles de Gaulle

The superior leader gets things done with very little
motion. He imparts instruction, not through many
words, but through few deeds. He keeps informed
about everything but interferes hardly at all. He is a
catalyst and though things would not get done quite
as well if he were not there, when they succeed, he
takes no credit, and because he takes no credit,
credit never leaves him.

Lao-tzu

A leader is a dealer in hope.

Napoleon Bonaparte

Great people hallow a whole people and lift up all
who live in their time.

Sydney Smith

A frightened captain makes a frightened crew.

Lister Sinclair

There is only one way to lead people and that is to be strong, because in strength there is no error, no illusion, it is the naked truth.

Napoleon Bonaparte

It is better to have a lion at the head of an army of sheep than a sheep at the head of an army of lions.

Daniel Defoe

I have always seen Richard as a figurehead. He was like the house captain at school; somebody that everyone admired and knew he was going places, and they would follow him if they could.

Mike Oldfield (of Richard Branson)

Ridiculous yachts and private planes and big limousines won't make people enjoy life more, and it sends out terrible messages to the people who work for them. It would be so much better if that money was spent in Africa – and it's about getting a balance.

Richard Branson

Chapter 12

The Knowledge

All the knowledge in the world, without action, will achieve nothing but will remain only as knowledge.

Richard Branson's private retreat – Necker Island in the British Virgin Islands was for sale at £3 million. Branson offered the owner only $250,000 US and purchased the property for $300,000. How? In short, he did some research and gained the knowledge that the vendor, Lord Cobham, was trying to raise funds to build a site for an educational trust. What is more he required the funds rather urgently. Branson gained the knowledge and acted upon it.

Deborah Meaden says, *"A critical point (in business) is research. It is so important to understand as much as you can about the market you're about to enter if you're going to minimise risk. Yes, being an entrepreneur is about taking risks but you can minimise risk by fully understanding what you are about to do."*

So where do you gain all this knowledge and information? Through quality research. By quality I do not mean through newspapers. It's a sad reality that for many people their post-school education about what is going on in the world around them comes from what they read in newspapers. What is most worrying is that a great many people are incredibly gullible and actually believe most of what they read. Friends of mine have been lied about in the press, and I have been lied about in the press, even by *The Guardian* and *The Telegraph* (although the worst one was the *Sunday Mirror*). You simply cannot believe anything you read in them. I no longer read them and there is a vast and growing number of people who also don't read them. It's hard to comprehend, for example, that some people still buy certain newspapers despite the awful lies they printed about the McCann family. What newspapers often write is opinion, conjecture and speculation and more often than you would believe, utter trash.

There are a great many sources of independent research, historical, scientific and business fact. Another great source of information, and one of the best, is yourself. Get out there and speak to people – see things and try things for yourself – and remember if you didn't hear it from the horse's mouth then there's every chance it's not fact. Remember there are two types of fiction, one comes from newspapers and one can be found in novels. If you want good fiction read a novel.

The most valuable commodity I know of is information.

Michael Douglas
(as Gordon Gekko in Oliver Stone's *'Wall Street'*)

The secret of business is to know something that nobody else knows.

Aristotle Onassis

Once a newspaper touches a story, the facts are lost forever, even to the protagonists.

Norman Mailer

Trying to determine what is going on in the world by reading a newspaper is like trying to tell the time by watching the second hand of a clock.

Ben Hecht

The man who reads nothing at all is better educated than the man who reads nothing but newspapers.

Thomas Jefferson

I have learned much more from conducting my own random surveys than I could ever have learned from the greatest consultancy firms.

Donald Trump

Knowledge is power.

Francis Bacon

Know thyself.

Socrates

All those who have turned out worth anything have had a chief hand in their own education.

Sir Walter Scott

Knowledge is of two kinds; we know a subject ourselves or we know where we can find information about it.

Samuel Johnson

I can learn a lot more going from door to door for three hours than I can from sitting in my office for three years.

William J Bressman

I have taken knowledge to be my province.

Francis Bacon

Knowledge dispels fear.

Motto of the Parachute School

How many a man has dated a new era in their lives from the reading of a book.

Thoreau

There are greater crimes than burning books. One of them is not reading them.

Joseph Brodsky

The ability to deal with people is as purchasable a commodity as sugar or coffee, and I will pay more for that knowledge.

John D Rockefeller

Chapter 13

Money Money Money

Alexander Dumas talked about something that had a profound effect on me and it really hit home when I began my overseas property project. OPM – it stands for Other People's Money, and I would say that it's one of the great secrets of success that isn't a secret at all. It's effectively what banks give you when you take out a loan or when you go into overdraft.

If you are starting out in business and have little or no capital and can't raise it, then you probably won't be able to produce a product en mass as stock, but as I mentioned earlier you should be getting orders before you produce a lot of stock. If you have got orders then go to the bank. It is sometimes best to sell or distribute something produced by others. However, as I said in the chapter on persuasion, choose your wares carefully and limit the choice to those you really believe in....

So you have a mortgage. Maybe you're in arrears or in a negative equity situation. You have bills like the rest of us, for sure, but can you afford to pay them? Perhaps you just pay them without giving it a second thought, in which case, well done, you're in the minority.

Are you one of those millions of people who save each year, for a whole year just to get a week or two in a cheap hotel on a Spanish Costa, and then have to budget daily with your very hard earned spending money? And then you come home to a pile of bills you can't pay? Most people fall exactly into that category. Now put your hand on your heart and tell me you are happy with that. Tell me you are happy, period. Do you believe that's your station in life? Do you accept it and just plod on? We are told that money can't buy happiness – absolute trash! Everyone is a unique individual and all their needs and wants differ greatly. Money *can* buy happiness. It would be better to say that it can't buy happiness for everyone, but it can for some people.

I've heard people supposedly quoting the bible saying 'Money is the route of all evil'. Now, as I said at the beginning, I'm not particularly religious, but I don't have to be to tell you that in the bible it actually says, 'The love of money is the route of all evil'. I can also tell you that there are many of the opinion that religion is the route of all evil but that's a very controversial subject for a different debate.

I have also heard some people saying things like 'who needs money', or 'money isn't the most important thing in the world'. I find the absurdity and stupidity of such statements leaving me, well, frankly stunned and numb with disbelief. Wake up folks – think about this very carefully, money buys food, clothing, puts a roof over our heads – yes, even the cardboard boxes that some very unfortunate homeless people have to sleep in, cost money, to someone, somewhere back down the line. It is money that pays for all hospitals and all health care, each and every charity in existence, transport, and countless other products and services on a near endless list. Money pays for just about everything everywhere, nearly all that is a basic need for the human race to survive, save for the air we breath and the sun. Why, people have even found ways to charge for those. The fact is, that unless we as a species are willing to go back to the days of the cavemen, then we need money. Even love costs money! Analyse that statement in its rudiments for just a moment, and as ridiculous as it may seem, you can't give love if you are not alive, and money, either directly or indirectly, keeps us all alive, except of course where there is the intervention of some event or illness. But even then, in many cases, money can indirectly prolong life. So believe me when I say, in the real world: MONEY *IS* THE MOST IMPORTANT THING IN THE WORLD. People should say: 'A lot of money isn't the most important thing in the world'.

Theo Paphitis says, *"Cash is King. Profit is sanity. Turnover is vanity. A lack of cash is like a heart attack for a business. If you can't pay the rent you shut down, just like you would if your heart packed up. You're finished. If you can't pay the wages it's all over. Don't be without cash. You can live without profit for a while, but not without cash. It's very basic and simple advice."*

Richard Branson pointed out that, "*I think that if you go out to get rich quickly, you probably won't succeed. But if you go out to do something that you really believe in and are passionate about, and if it's a good idea and you stick at it, then you probably will succeed. Then the financial rewards will come.*"

People who say that money isn't the most important thing in the world are usually broke.

Malcolm Forbes

I enjoy living like a poor man, but with lots of money.

Pablo Piccasso

I've been rich and I've been poor and believe me when I say – rich is better.

Sophie Tucker

Money makes money and the money, money makes, makes more money.

Benjamin Franklin

Profit is not a natural condition, it requires special work to create.

Bill Gates

You direct a garage or another business like you drive a bus. It does its round, stopping to pick people up. But it can't make a long distance trip, and of course some can be happy driving the same route all their lives. But I wanted to drive bigger, faster and better buses and see more places.

Soichiro Honda

With money in your pocket; you are wise, you are handsome, and you sing well too.

Jewish Proverb

Money can say more in one minute than the most eloquent lover can in years.

Henry Fielding

One hundred thousand Francs or one hundred million Francs, it's all the same to me.

Aristotle Onassis

If you're short, take a loan. Never ask for a small amount. Ask for what you need and always pay it back. The sooner the better.

Aristotle Onassis

Money is like an arm or a leg, you either use it or lose it.

Henry Ford

Money is the most important thing in the world!!!

The author

Chapter 14

The Great Lies

It's a sad reality that so many people's lives are governed it seems, by the strangest of doctrines, the most defeatist of philosophies. Do you think that it is purely coincidence that the vast majority and probably all of these people are not what you and I might call successful? I very much doubt whether any of those whose thoughts feature in this book could ever have amassed their vast fortunes or achieved their successes had they lived their lives by such beliefs.

"The meek shall inherit the earth."
But not the mineral rights replied John Paul Getty.

"You can't have your cake and eat it."
Try telling that to a self-made millionaire.

"All good things come to those who wait."
So does death!

"Know your limitations."
If you truly believe you have limitations then you have failed before you have even begun.

"By and by, pie in the sky, when you die."
Most people want their pie now, down on the ground while they're still around and they want ice cream, maple syrup and a cherry on top.

"Some people were just born lucky."
Personally I don't believe in pure luck. I think we create our own. It comes in the beginning as opportunity, and of course whether or not we take those opportunities is up to us. You can't have 'luck of the draw' unless you enter the draw.

"One day my ship will come in."
Wake up! Your ship has been in port for years, just waiting for you to unload it.

Chapter 15

Lighten Up!

A bank is a place where they lend you an umbrella in fair weather and then take it a away again when it begins to rain.

Robert Frost

I'm not afraid of dying, it's just that I don't want to be there when it happens.

Woody Allen

I was once so poor, I didn't know where my next husband was coming from.

Mae West

Divorce, is when a husband no longer has to take the money home to his wife, he can mail it.

Monty Croft

I have a lovely wife and family, a dog and a bank manager to support.

Eric Morecambe

I once said cynically of a politician – he'll double cross that bridge when he comes to it.

Oscar Levant

Only one man in a thousand is a leader of men. The other 999 follow women.

Groucho Marx

A government is the only known vessel which leaks from the top.

Author unknown

A committee is a gathering of important people who singularly can do nothing and together can decide that nothing can be done.

Fred Allen

A good politician is quite as unthinkable as an honest burglar.

H L Mencken

If you're given a choice between money and sex appeal, take the money. As you get older, the money will become your sex appeal.

Katharine Hepburn

Dolphins are so intelligent that within a few days of captivity, they have trained humans to stand at the side of a pool and throw fish to them.

Author unknown

I find television very educating. Every time someone turns a set on I go into another room and read a book.

Groucho Marx

What's the quickest way to become a millionaire? Borrow fivers off everyone you meet.

Richard Branson

When I was young I used to think that money was the most important thing in life; now that I am old, I know it is.

Oscar Wilde

A FINAL MESSAGE FROM THE AUTHOR

Whatever your background, whatever your race, or colour of your skin, whatever nationality or religion you hold, however physically unattractive or attractive your are and whatever ability or disability you are gifted with, you have as equal a right to monetary wealth or any other form of success as any other human being on the face of the earth, and should that right be denied you, then you must fight for that right.

The only thing that matters is that your achievements are gained through righteous means. We all make mistakes in life, travel down wrong roads, take wrong turns, and for the wrong reasons. The person who claims to be free of these faults and then judges others is nothing more and nothing less than a puritanical hypocrite.

With every moment in every day comes the seed of new opportunity. A fresh chance to do something, anything, as long as it's the right thing. I have only one request of you. Reach your heady heights of greatness in any manner you wish so long as you do not bring failure or damage to others in the process.

Finally I would like to suggest to you that the greatness of a rich human being is not measured by the size of their bank balance, but rather by what they do with it.

Selected Who's Who

As you have probably gathered, not all those quoted in this book are billionaire entrepreneurs. However some are accumulating millions at an astonishing rate. Many of them have had successes in other fields – sports, politics, art, literature etc. They have attained self satisfaction and at the very least, relative financial security. Some of them lived thousands of years ago yet their names are as indelibly scribed in our present as in their day, if not more so. Whatever their chosen fields are, or were, and whether you admire them or not, one thing is for certain; they are all ACHIEVERS!

Woody Allen
Controversial US film director, actor and writer.

Jay Abraham
One of the US's highest paid marketing consultants. Has helped more than 10,000 businesses and has earned more than $20 million in the process.

Stella Adler
One of the chief influences in the screen acting method of numerous brilliant screen actors including Robert De Niro.

Mary Kay Ash
Founder of the very successful Mary Kay Cosmetics.

Fred Allen
Head of Pitney Bowes.

Duncan Bannatyne
Amassed well over two hundred million pounds. Started at the age of thirty with a single old ice cream van. Diverse interests from care homes to casinos. One of the stars of the TV series Dragons' Den.

William Blake
18th century English artist. Principal work *'Dante meeting Beatrice in Paradise'*.

Napoleon Bonaparte
French emperor – early 19th century.

Sir Richard Branson
High profile and flamboyant founder and chairman of the Virgin Group. From ground zero, he built this international empire encompassing two hundred diverse interests to make him one the richest people in Britain.

William J Bressman
Head of teleprompter (cable division).

Andrew Carnagie
Billionaire Scottish industrialist with Charles Schwab and others, he formed the United States Steel Corporation during the early 1900s.

Lord Chesterfield
Journalist, statesman, speaker and author during the 18ᵗʰ century.

Winston Churchill
British Prime Minister.

George Coleman
British Prime Minister.

Confucius
Chinese philosopher – d.479 bc.

Sir Sean Connery
From 0 to 007. Scottish international film star. Became famous as Ian Fleming's James Bond. One of the most enduring screen actors ever. Some of his better works in his filmography include, *'Medicine Man'*, *'Finding Forrester'* and *'The Russia House'*.

Daniel Defoe
British author, journalist and poet.

Benjamin Disraeli
British Prime Minster during the 19ᵗʰ century.

Alexander Dumas
French writer.

R W Emerson
US poet and essayist.

Albert Einstein
German American physicist famous mainly for his theory of relativity.

F Scott Fitzgerald
Author of *'The Great Gatsby'* and *'This Side of Paradise'*.

Malcolm Forbes
Editor in Chief of Forbes magazine – sold worldwide.

Henry Ford
Pioneer of the automobile, and industrialist.

Jodie Foster
Critically acclaimed international film star. *'Nell'*, *'The Accused'*, *'The Silence of the Lambs'*, *'Contact'* etc.

Bill Gates
Co-founder of Microsoft in his late teens. By far the richest man in the world and entirely self made. At one point wealth estimated at $50 billion.

John Paul Getty
Multi billionaire, led a mainly reclusive life. Getty senior struck oil and founded the Getty Oil Company. Getty junior inherited. Grandson Mark Getty now at the helm.

Joe Girard
Entered the Guinness Book of Records as the world's greatest salesman. Main line of business – car sales. He achieved 13,001 individual (not fleet) vehicle sales in 15 years. In 1973 alone he sold 1425, around 119 per month.

James Goldsmith
Colourful billionaire, financier and founder of the Referendum Party.

Sam Goldwyn
The G in MGM (Metro Goldwyn Meyer) and a pioneer of the Hollywood motion picture industry.

Al Gore
Former US vice president and presidential candidate.

Napoleon Hill
Author of 'Think and Grow Rich' with sales in excess of 7 million.

Soshiro Honda
Founder of the Honda Motor Company.

Victor Kiam
'It'll shave you as close as a blade or I'll give you your money back' the famous slogan of the Remington company he bought.

Arnold Kopleson
Highly successful film producer including *'Seven'*, *'The Fugitive'*, *'Platoon'*.

Ray Kroc
Purchased a single hamburger stall from the McDonald's brothers at age 55. Transformed that single enterprise into probably the world's most famous household name in fast food.

Estée Lauder
Founded Estée Lauder Cosmetics. Began by parlaying a face cream that was concocted by her uncle from Hungary.

Groucho Marx
US actor and comic.

Molière
French actor and movie star.

Eric Morecambe
British comedian famous from the duo Morecambe and Wise.

Aristotle Onassis
Was the household name in Greek shipping. Began selling neck ties on the streets in South America. He rose quickly to a flamboyant lifestyle and gained numerous famous friends including royalty from various countries. Onassis was a grafter and never

forgot where he came from. Immortalised on screen by Anthony Quinn in a movie of his life.

Theo Paphitis

Retail magnate with such brands as Contessa and Ryman. Shot to fame as a member of BBC's Dragons' Den.

H Ross Perot

Multi billionaire and former presidential candidate. His wealth includes large amounts of cash built up with real estate, oil and gas exploration.

Pablo Picasso

Spanish painter of the Cubist school. Prolific period was early to mid 20th century.

Mario Puzo

Author of numerous books including the hugely successful 'Godfather' trilogy starring such great screen talents as Robert De Niro, Al Pacino, Marlon Brando, James Caan and Robert Duvall.

Anthony Robbins

US success guru. Hosts worldwide sell-out seminars at $ thousands per ticket.

John D Rockefeller

Billionaire financier and industrialist. Founder of Standard Oil.

Anita Roddick
Founder of The Body Shop. Started with a private loan of a few thousand pounds and built on her vision. The man who gave her that loan in the mid '70s did so for 50% of the company. 25 years later there are over 1700 branches of The Body Shop worldwide.

David Sainsbury
Sainsbury's.

Socrates
Ancient Greek philosopher and teacher of Plato.

Steven Spielberg
Possibly the most successful film director in the world, also highly successful writer and producer. Works include 'Jaws', 'Close Encounters of the Third Kind', 'Indiana Jones' and 'Jurassic Park' trilogies, 'Schindlers List' etc, etc.

Oliver Stone
Controversial film director/writer responsible for 'Platoon', 'JFK' and 'Wall Street' etc.

Alan Sugar
Alan Michael Sugar trading as Amstrad.

Recommended Reading

SCREW IT, LETS DO IT
Richard Branson

TALK AND GROW RICH
Ron Holland

THINK AND GROW RICH
Napoleon Hill

**HOW TO WIN FRIENDS
AND INFLUENCE PEOPLE**
Dale Carnegie

**KINESICS
THE POWER OF SILENT COMMAND**
Merlyn Cundiff

INSTANT ADVERTISING
Bradley J Sugars

ANYONE CAN DO IT
Duncan Bannatyne

ENTER THE DRAGON
Theo Paphitis

THE ART OF THE DEAL
Donald Trump with Tony Schwartz

Action Notes

Use the following note pages to write down your ideas, what you are going to do about them and when.

_____

_____

_____

_____

_____

_____

_____

_____

_____

_____

_____

_____

About the Author

John Lanasis was born in Glasgow. The son of a Greek father and an Irish mother, he has lived and travelled extensively in Europe, was educated privately at an Anglo-American School in Athens and studied creative advertising and marketing at college. He speaks Greek and some Italian.

John has set up and successfully run three small businesses, achieved a company sales record in property for a major UK estate agency chain and was solely responsible for breaking two sales records in the travel business in Greece. He has assisted a number small companies to develop new brand identities, creative advertising concepts and to improve their front line image.

John is passionate about creativity and from that perspective is a member of British Actors Equity, and BAFTA – the British Academy of Film and Television Arts. He trained as a drama director at the BBC and between entrepreneurial and other pursuits, continues to engage in professional work in film and TV.

He has been published as a writer and a photographer with a character photographic book on the Greek island of Corfu due for publication in the near future.

John mainly divides his time between the UK and Corfu where he owns a villa.

You can contact John Lanasis either via the website www.newpowerbooks.co.uk or email johnlanasis1@mac.com